MW00882096

We would also like to send out a big thank you to:

- MTsamples.com for the use of some of their dictation and operative notes.
- The ASC review for their coding guidance article by the American Medical Association.
- Ingenix for their insight and guidance provided in their "Coder's Desk Reference" and their ICD-9-CM Expert Edition manual.
- The AMA for their valuable insights provided in the CPT Professional Edition manual.
- The members and experts in the AAPC forums who are continually handing out good professional coding advice.
- The AAPC Local Norwalk Chapter in Ohio for providing their advice, insight, and time proofreading and editing the exam.

THANK YOU!

Table of Contents

Congratulations!

You have taken a major step toward your CPC certification.

This 150 question CPC practice exam has been constructed to reflect the actual CPC exam as closely as possible. You will find that each question and its answers closely emulate those on the actual CPC exam. The layout of the exam is also the layout you can expect to see on exam day.

For the best results we suggest the following:

1) Read through this CPC Exam Study Guide, including the Common Anatomy Terms and Medical Terminology handouts **located right after the Study Guide**.
2) Read and study this entire packet prior to starting the CPC practice exam.
3) Locate the Scantron Bubble Sheets where you will note down your answers to the 150 questions.
4) Read the Proctor-to-Coder Instructions **just prior** to taking the examination.
5) When taking the exam set aside a 5 hour and 40 minute block of time in a quiet, distraction free, environment and attempt taking the exam all at once.
6) Have two or three sharpened #2 pencils, an eraser, a blank sheet of scrap paper, a calculator, your three coding manuals, and the CPC practice exam.
7) Take a long break before trying to grade the exam and comprehend the rationale. You may want to choose someone else grade the answers and give you your results, and then later sit down with the rationale.

The idea is that you should create a practice environment that closely simulates taking the real CPC exam. That way you won't feel flustered or overwhelmed when taking the test for real – you will recognize the setting and can focus on your goal, **passing the CPC**!

Sincerely,

Gunnar Bengtsson

Gunnar Bengtsson, medicalbillingandmedicalcoding.com

Study and Exam Preparation Guide

The first step in exam preparation is knowing and re-checking your coding manuals. Since the majority of the CPC exam is focused on the CPT coding manual we too will focus on this manual during preparation.

CPT Manual:

Front Cover: Common coding conventions (symbols) are listed here. Coding modifiers with a short description are listed here. HCPCS modifiers that approved for CPT Level I use are listed here with a short description as well.

Introduction: These are located only a few pages in from the front cover and are labeled with roman numerals instead of page numbers. The introduction should be read at least once. Highlighting and notations are allowed and suggested.

References: Following the introduction there are a few pages with common medical prefixes, suffixes, root words, directions, positions, and anatomical terms. This page should be tabbed for easy use during the exam. Terms not already listed on these pages can be hand written in. Using the common medical anatomy terms and medical terminology handouts provided with this packet, transfer unknown terms to these pages in your CPT book.

Following the common terminology pages are a few pages listing where anatomical illustrations can be found in your CPT manual. This is followed by three diagrams of the body planes and aspects. The location of these pages should also be noted (or tabbed).

General Layout: The CPT book has a general layout that it follows. The manual is divided into chapters that are organ system specific (ex. Integumentary, Respiratory, Etc.) Chapters are listed in numerical order with the exception of E/M codes (which start with 99). Each chapter has chapter specific coding guidelines listing prior to their code sets. The general coding guidelines for each chapter should be read at least once. Highlighting and notations are allowed and suggested. Avoid highlighting common words and phrases and try to highlight specific guidelines and rules.

Following general coding guidelines are the codes sets, which may or may not have code specific coding guidelines.

Code sets are generally listed in an anatomical order. This means that codes pertaining to the outside of the body are listed and progress inward, and codes pertaining to the top of the body are listed first and progress downward. Example: in the respiratory system the codes pertaining to the nose start with the outside of the nose (skin) and progress to the inside and eventually to the sinuses (outside inward). Codes pertaining to the nose are all listed before codes pertaining to the lungs (top to bottom). Each chapter follows this type of layout.

General Coding Rules: All CPT codes have a common descriptor, a unique descriptor, or both.
A common descriptor is a description that applies to more than one CPT code and it is located prior to the semi-colon (;). The unique descriptor is a description that applies to a single CPT code and is located after the semi-colon (;)

Unique descriptors are indented beneath a common descriptor beside their CPT code.

Example:

12001 Simple repair of a superficial wound of scalp, neck, axillae, external genitalia, trunck and/or extremities (including hands and feet); 2.5cm or less

12002   2.6cm to 7.5cm

12004   7.6cm to 12.5cm

CPT codes may also have notations beneath them indicating specific coding guidelines, such as a code it may not be used in conjunction with, sequencing, etc.

Coding conventions may be located to the left of a CPT code also indicating a specific coding guideline. A short description of the convention's meaning can be found at the bottom of each page and a full description can be found in the introduction at the beginning of the CPT manual.

Following the chapters that contain category I codes are two indexes containing category II and category III codes. Category II codes are tracking codes used for performance and quality measures. Category III codes end in the letter T and are temporary codes used for new emerging technology, services, and procedures.

Following the category II and III codes are Appendix A - N. Each appendix is useful in its own way, but for the examination we suggest reading and knowing the locations of appendix A (modifiers and their full descriptions and guidelines), appendix D (a list of all add on codes), appendix E (a list of all modifier 51 exempt codes), appendix F (modifier 63 exempt codes), appendix G (codes that include conscious sedation), appendix K (codes with products pending FDA approval), appendix L (vascular families), and appendix N (a list of re-sequenced codes).

Following the appendices is the alphabetic index.

The back cover of the CPT manual contained common medical abbreviations.

ICD-9-CM Manual:

ICD-9-CM manuals vary depending on who the publisher is but all should contain an introduction in the beginning of the manual. The introduction should contain steps to correct coding, including convention descriptions and proper use.

General coding guidelines should follow the introduction and chapter specific coding guidelines should follow general coding guidelines.

Important things to know regarding ICD-9-CM conventions and coding guidelines include (but are not limited to):

- Meanings of NEC and NOS
- Definitions and proper use of brackets [ ], Parentheses ( ), and colons :
- Proper use of the following notations:
    - Includes
        - Excludes
        - "other specified" codes
        - "unspecified" codes
        - "Code first"
        - "use additional code"
        - "in diseases classified elsewhere"
        - "and"
        - "with"
        - "see" and "see also"
- You must always utilize a code to its fullest available digit (if a code has four digits all four must be used, if a code has five digits all five must be used. Etc.)
- Rules regarding:
    - Signs and Symptoms
    - Coding Manifestations
    - Code Sequencing
    - Combination Coding
    - Coding Late Effects
- Always verify a code in the tabular index.
- Read three-digit category coding guidelines and look for code specific coding guidelines and notations beneath specific codes.

Things to Remember

- Diagnostic endoscopies that turn into procedural endoscopies become bundled with the procedural code and cannot be coded separately
- Modifier 51 is generally added to all secondary procedure codes unless the code is modifier 51 exempt

- Modifiers do are not appended to ICD-9-CM codes, only to CPT (level I) and HCPCS (level II) codes.
- E codes are always coded last in sequencing and they are never coded alone.
- "Probable", "Suspected, "Rule Out", and similarly worded diagnosis should not be coded in an outpatient setting.

General Test Taking Tips

- Answer the easy questions first and skip the long ones. Each question is worth the same amount of points and the long ones take up time to read. Just remember to also skip the answer on the bubble sheet.
- Start the exam with the chapter you are most knowledgeable in, even if that means staring in the middle of the exam.
- Skip using the alphabetic index during the exam. Instead, take the four answers that are provided to you and look them up directly in the tabular index.
- Follow your first instinct. Statistics show that when an individual comes back to a previously answered question and changes their answer they often had the correct answer and changed it to the wrong one.
- At some point everyone runs into a question they just do not know the answer for. Never leave an answer blank because even a guess will give you a 25% chance of getting it correct.
- When making a guess try to make an educated one based on logic.
    - Often the correct answer (code) will be repeated in at least two of the four options. An answer with a code that does not appear in any of the other options can often be ruled out as the correct answer.
    - The answer often corresponds to the chapter that is being tested. For example, if you are in the "respiratory" chapter questions the answer will most likely contain a 30000 code. Answers that have codes from other chapters (ex. A digestive code; 50000 series) can most likely be ruled out as the correct answer
    - Often a modifier will be appended to two of the four options. If you can determine if the modifier is appropriate or not you

can usually narrow down your options from four to two (giving you a 50% chance of guessing the correct answer).

- According to the AAPC Exam Proctors Sheet which is distributed by the AAPC to the exam proctors, "Tabs can be inserted, taped, pasted, glued or stapled in the manuals, if the obvious intent is to earmark a page with words or numbers and not add supplemental information. No other material of any kind may be taped stapled or glued into the manuals to be used during the examination. Handwritten notes in coding books (as those commonly seen in daily work coding activities) are permitted. Manuals will not be disqualified due to writing contained therein".
  - o Additional anatomy labels such on the provided diagrams are useful. An example would be to label the Incus, Malleus, and Stapes (in the auditory system) with their common names the Anvil, Hammer, and Stirrup.

Common Anatomy Terms

Directional Terms:

Anterior (ventral) – Toward the front of the body

Central – At or near the center of the body or organ

Distal – Part of an extremity that is farther from the point of attachment to the trunk

External (superficial) – Toward or on the surface of the body

Inferior (caudad) – Away from the head

Internal – Away from the surface of the body

Lateral – Away from the midline of the body

Medial – Toward the midline of the body

Parietal – Pertaining to the outer boundary of body cavities

Peripheral – External to or away from the center of the body or organ

Posterior (dorsal) – Toward the back of the body

Proximal – Part of an extremity that is closer to the point of attachment to the trunk

Superior (cephalad) – Toward the head

Visceral – Pertaining to the internal organs

Planes:

Frontal Plane – (AKA: Coronal Plane) Is an imaginary line that runs vertically across the shoulders, sides, and hips to divide the body from front to back

Midsagittal Plane – (AKA: Sagittal Plane or Lateral Plane) Is an imaginary line that runs vertically down the spine, face, and center of the abdomen to divide the body into left and right portions.

Transverse Plane – (AKA: Cross–Sectional Plane) imaginary line that runs horizontally through the abdomen (at the naval) and through the back to divide the body into top and bottom.

Body Cavities:

Abdominopelvic Cavity – A subdivision of the ventral cavity which encases the abdominal cavity and pelvic cavity.

Dorsal Cavity – A body cavity which encases the cranial cavity and vertebral canal.

Thoracic Cavity – A subdivision of the ventral cavity which is located in the chest and encases the mediastinum, pleural cavity, and pericardial cavity

Ventral Cavity – A cavity that encases the thoracic cavity, the diaphragm, and the abdominopelvic cavity abdomen (at the naval) and through the back to divide the body into top and bottom.

Abdominopelvic Quadrants:

Left Upper Quadrant (LUQ) – One of the four quadrants that the abdominopelvic area can be divided into. Located in the left upper portion of the abdomen it includes a view of the stomach, spleen, the left kidney, and parts of the duodenum, pancreas, left ureter, small intestine, and transverse and descending colon.

Left Lower Quadrant (LLQ) – One of the four quadrants that the abdominopelvic area can be divided into. Located in the left lower portion of the abdominopelvic area and provides partial views of the small intestine, descending and sigmoid colon, rectum, left ureter, and urinary bladder.

Right Lower Quadrant (RLQ) – One of the four quadrants that the abdominopelvic area can be divided into. Located in the right lower portion of the abdominopelvic area and includes a view of the appendix, cecum, and partial views of the ascending colon, small intestine, right ureter, urinary bladder, and rectum.

Right Upper Quadrant (RUQ) – One of the four quadrants that the abdominopelvic area can be divided into. Located in the right upper portion of the abdomen it provides a view of the gallbladder, most of the liver, and partial views of the pancreas, small intestine, and ascending and transverse colon.

Abdominopelvic Regions :

Epigastic Region – One of the six regions the abdominopelvic cavity can be divided into. It is located in the center of the upper abdomen just below the sternum. It includes partial views of the liver, stomach, pancreas, duodenum, and transverse colon.

Hypogastric Region – One of the six regions the abdominopelvic cavity can be divided into. It is located the center of the lower pelvis between the hips. It includes a view of the urinary bladder and rectum, and partial views of the ureters, small intestine, and sigmoid colon.

Left Hypochondriac Region – One of the six regions the abdominopelvic cavity can be divided into. It is located in the upper left abdomen and includes the floating rib cage. It provides a view of the spleen, and partial views of the stomach, transverse colon, and left kidney.

Left Iliac Region – One of the six regions the abdominopelvic cavity can be divided into. It is located in the left lower pelvic area and includes the left acetabulum. It provides partial views of the small intestine, and descending and sigmoid colon.

Left Lumbar Region – One of the six regions the abdominopelvic cavity can be divided into. It is located to the left of the naval and provides a view of the descending colon and partial views of the left kidney and small intestine.

Right Hypochondriac Region – One of the six regions the abdominopelvic cavity can be divided into. It is located in the upper right abdomen and includes the floating rib cage. It provides a view of the gallbladder, and partial views of the liver, transverse colon, and right kidney.

Right Iliac Region – One of the six regions the abdominopelvic cavity can be divided into. It is located in the right lower pelvic area and includes the right acetabulum. It provides a view of the appendix and cecum and a partial of the small intestine.

Right Lumbar Region – One of the six regions the abdominopelvic cavity can be divided into. It is located to the right of the naval and provides a view of the ascending colon and partial views of the small intestine and right kidney.

Umbilical Region – One of the six regions the abdominopelvic cavity can be divided into. It is located directly in the center of the abdominopelvic cavity and provides a partial view of the duodenum, small intestine, kidneys, and ureters.

Regions of the Head and Neck:

Cephalic – The head. Contain smaller facial and cranial regions.

Cervical – The neck.

Cranial – The part of the head containing the brain.

Facial – The face.

Regions of the Trunk

Abdominal – The region located between the lowest ribs and the hip bones.

Abdominopelvic – Contains both the abdominal and pelvic regions.

Axillary – The armpits

Coxal – The hips

Dorsum – The posterior surface of the thorax

Genital – The external reproductive organs

Gluteal – The buttocks

Inguinal –The groin

Lumbar – The lower back

Pectoral –The chest

Perineal – The small region between the anus and the external reproductive organs.

Pelvic – The region enclosed by the pelvic bones.

Sacral – The region over the sacrum and between the buttocks.

Sternal – The region over the breast bone.

Vertebral – The region over the back bone.

Medical Terminology: Prefixes

- Prefix: a–
  Meaning: Without
  Example: Amenorrhea – without a menstruation cycle

- Prefix: ab– , abs–
  Meaning: away from
  Example: Abrade – to wear away

- Prefix: ad–
  Meaning: toward, to
  Example: Addiction –involuntary dependence upon a substance or action

- Prefix: ambi–
  Meaning: both, around
  Example: Ambidextrous – having ability on both sides

- Prefix: an–
  Meaning: Without
  Example: Anorexia – without appetite

- Prefix: ana–
  Meaning: up, toward
  Example: Anaphylactic – exaggerated reaction to an antigen or toxin

- Prefix: ante–
  Meaning: before
  Example: Antepartum – before labor or childbirth

- Prefix:anti–
  Meaning: against
  Example: Antidepressant – counteracting depression

- Prefix: apo–
  Meaning: derived, separate
  Examples: apodia – congenital absence of feet

- Prefix: auto(o)–
  Meaning: self
  Example: autogenous – originating within the body

- Prefix: bi–
  Meaning: twice, double
  Example: bilobular – having two lobes

- Prefix: brachy–
  Meaning: short
  Example: brachymelia – disproportionate shortness of limbs

- Prefix: brady–
  Meaning: Slow
  Example: bradypepsia – slowness of digestion

- Prefix: cata–
  Meaning: Down
  Example: catabolism – breaking down of chemicals in the body

- Prefix: circum–
  Meaning: around
  Example: circumcision – cutting around the male genitalia

- Prefix: co–; col–; com–; con–; cor–
  Meaning: together
  Example: collaboration – to bring together the efforts of two or more people

- Prefix: contra–
  Meaning: against
  Example: contraceptive – to protect against conception

- Prefix: de–
  Meaning: away from
  Example: delivery – the passage of fetus and placenta away from the genital canal into the external world

- Prefix: di–; dif–; dir–; dis–
  Meaning: not, separated
  Example: Dislocation – separation of a joint

- Prefix: dia–
  Meaning: through
  Example: dialysis – blood filtration through artificial kidney function

- Prefix: dys–
  Meaning: abnormal, difficult
  Example: Dysuria – difficult urination

- Prefix: ect(o)–
  Meaning: outside
  Example: ectocyst – outer layer of a hydatid cyst

- Prefix: end(o)–
  Meaning: within
  Example: endoscopy – examination of the interior with a scope

- Prefix: epi–
  Meaning: over
  Example: Epidemic – widespread disease over large geographical areas

- Prefix: eu–
  Meaning: well, good, normal
  Example: eutherapeutic – having excellent curative properties

- Prefix: ex–
  Meaning: out of, away from
  Example: excretion – to pass out of the body

- Prefix: exo–
  Meaning: external, on the outside
  Example: Exocrine – a type of gland that secretes onto the surface of the body

- Prefix: extra–
  Meaning: without, outside of
  Example: extraoral – outside or the oral cavity

- Prefix: hemi-
  Meaning: half
  Example: Hemiplegia – paralysis on one side of the body

- Prefix: hyper-
  Meaning: above normal, overly
  Example: Hyperglycemia – high blood sugar

- Prefix: hypo-
  Meaning: below normal
  Example: Hypoglycemia – low blood sugar

- Prefix: infra-
  Meaning: positioned beneath
  Example: infrapatellar – beneath the patella

- Prefix: inter-
  Meaning: between
  Example: internal – beneath the surface

- Prefix: intra-
  Meaning: within
  Example: intranasal – within the nasal cavity

- Prefix: iso-
  Meaning: equal, same
  Example: isolate – to separate and set apart from others

- Prefix: mal-
  Meaning: bad, inadequate
  Example: maladie – a disease or illness

- Prefix: meg(a)- megal(o)-
  Meaning: large
  Example: Megalocardia – enlarged heart

- Prefix: mes(o) –
  Meaning: middle, median
  Example: Mesoderm – the middle layer of skin

- Prefix: meta-
  Meaning: after
  Example: metatarsal – the foot bone after the tarsal bone

- Prefix: micr(o)-
  Meaning: small, microscopic
  Example: microscopic – minutely small and invisible to the unaided eye

- Prefix: mon(o)-
  Meaning: single
  Example: Monolocular – having one cavity or chamber

- Prefix: multi-
  Meaning: many
  Examples: multinodular – having many nodes

- Prefix: olig(o)-
  Meaning: few, little, scanty
  Example: oligodipsia – abnormal lack of thirst

- Prefix: pan-, pant(o)-
  Meaning: all, entire
  Example: panacea – cure all remedy

- Prefix: per-
  Meaning: through, intensely
  Example: percutaneous – passage of substance through the skin

- Prefix: pluri-
  Meaning: several, more
  Example: pluriresistant – having multiple aspects of resistance

- Prefix: poly-
  Meaning: many
  Example: polyadentitis – inflammation of many lymph nodes

- Prefix: post-
  Meaning: after, following
  Example: Posterior – the back surface of the body

- Prefix: pre-
  Meaning: before
  Example: Prenatal – before birth

- Prefix: pro-
  Meaning: before, forward
  Example: process – the projection, growth, or the action of moving forward

- Prefix: quadra-, quadri-
  Meaning: four
  Example: Quadrant – one fourth of a circle

- Prefix: re-
  Meaning: again, backward
  Example: reaction – to render active again

- Prefix: retro-
  Meaning: behind, backward
  Example: Retroflexion – bending backwards

- Prefix: semi-
  Meaning: half
  Example: Semicomatose – a state of half consciousness

- Prefix: sub-
  Meaning: under, inferior
  Example: Subcutaneous – beneath the skin

- Prefix: super-
  Meaning: more than, above, superior
  Example: supersonic – greater than the speed of sound

- Prefix: supra-
  Meaning: above, over
  Example: supraanal – above the anus

- Prefix: syl-, sym-, syn-, sys-
  Meaning: together
  Example: Symbiosis – mutual interdependence

- Prefix: tachy-
  Meaning: fast
  Example: Tachycardia – rapid heartbeat

- Prefix: trans-
  Meaning: across, through
  Example: transplant – to transfer from one part to another

- Prefix: ultra-
  Meaning: beyond, excessive
  Example: ultrasonic – sound waves at higher frequencies than sound

- Prefix: un-
  Meaning: not
  Example: unconscious – not conscious

- Prefix: uni-
  Meaning: one
  Example: union – joining of two parts into one

Medical Terminology: Root Words

- Root word: Acanth(o)
  Meaning: Spiny, thorny
  Example: acanthion – the tip of the anterior nasal spine

- Root word: Actin(o)
  Meaning: Light
  Example: Actinotherapy – ultraviolet light therapy used in dermatology

- Root word: Aer(o)
  Meaning: Air, gas
  Example: Aerosol – liquid or particulate matter dispersed in air, gas, or vapor form

- Root word: Alge, algesi, algio, algo
  Meaning: Pain
  Example: Analgesic – a pain reducing agent

- Root word: Amyl(o)
  Meaning: Starch
  Example: Amylolysis – hydrolysis of starch unto soluable products

- Root words: Andro
  Meaning: Masculine
  Example: Androsterone – a steroid metabolite found in male urine

- Root words: Athero
  Meaning: Plaque, fatty substance
  Example: Atheroembolism – cholesterol embolism originating from an atheroma

- Root qord: Bacill(i)
  Meaning: Bacilli, bacteria
  Example: Bacillemia – presence of bacilli in the blood

- Root word: Bacteri(o)
  Meaning: Bacteria
  Example: Bacteriocin – a protien toxin produced and released by bacteria

- Root word: Bar(o)
  Meaning: Weight, pressure
  Example: Bartaxis – reaction of living tissue to changes in pressure

- Root words: Bas(o), basi(o)
  Meaning: Base
  Example: Basoplasm – part of cytoplasm that stains readily with basic dyes

- Root words: Bio–
  Meaning: Life
  Example: Biopsy – sampling of tissue from living patients

- Root words: Blast(o)
  Meaning: Immature cells
  Example: blastoma – a neoplasm composed of immature cells

- Root words: Cac(o)
  Meaning: Bad, ill
  Example: cacomelia – congenital deformity of one or more limbs

- Root words: Calc(o), calci(o)
  Meaning: Calcium
  Example: Calcipenia – a condition of insufficient calcium

- Root words:Carcin(o)
  Meaning: Cancer
  Example: Carcinogen – cancer–producing substance

- Root words: Chem (o)
  Meaning: Chemical
  Example: Chemotherapy – the treatment of disease by the use of chemicals

- Root words: Chlor (o)
  Meaning: Chlorine, Green
  Example: Chloropenia – a deficiency in chloride

- Root words: Chondrio, Chondro
  Meaning: Cartilage, grainy, gritty
  Example: Chondropathy – ant diese of the cartilage

- Root words: Chore (o)
  Meaning: Dance
  Example: Choreoathetosis – abnormal body movements

- Root word: Chrom, Chromat, Chromo
  Meaning: Color
  Example: Chromatism – abnormal pigmentation

- Root word: Chrono
  Meaning: Time
  Example: Chonopharmicology – the study of the effects of drugs based on the timing of biological events and cycles.

- Root word: Chyl (o)
  Meaning: Chyle, digestive juice
  Example: Chylidrosis – sweating of milky fluid that resembles chyle

- Root word: Chym (o)
  Meaning: Chyme, semifluid produced of chyl and partially digested food
  Example: Chymorrhe – the flow of chyme

- Root word: Cine (o)
  Meaning: Movement
  Example: Cineradiography – the radiography of an organism on motion

- Root word: Coni (o)
  Meaning: Dust
  Example: Coniosis – any disease or morbid condition caused by dust

- Root word: Crin (o)
  Meaning: Secrete
  Example: Crinin – an old term for a substance that stimulates the production of secretion by specific glands

- Root word: Cry (o)
  Meaning: Cold
  Example: Cryospasm – movement of muscles caused by cold

- Root word: Crypt (o)
  Meaning: Hidden, Obscure
  Example: Cryptorchidism – failure of one or both testicals to descend

- Root word: Cyan (o)
  Meaning: Blue
  Example: Cyanosis – a darkblue or purplish color to the skin or mucous membranes

- Root word: Cycl (o)
  Meaning: Circle, Cycle, Cilliary body
  Example: Cyclectomy – excision of a portion of a ciliary body

- Root word: Cyst, Cyst (o)
  Meaning: Bladder, Cyst, Cystic duct
  Example: Cystitis – inflammation of the urinary bladder

- Root word: Cyt (o)
  Meaning: Cell
  Example: Cytocidal – causing the death of cells

- Root word: Dextr (o)
  Meaning: Right, toward right
  Example: Dexter – leaning toward or relating to the right side

- Root word: Dips (o)
  Meaning: Thirsty
  Example: Polydipsia – excessively thirsty

- Root word: Dors (o), dorsi
  Meaning: Back
  Example: Dorsolumbar – the lower back

- Root word: Dynamo
  Meaning: Force, energy
  Example: Dynamogenic – Power produced by muscular and neural activity

- Root word: Echo
  Meaning: Reflected sound
  Example: Echographer – an ultrasonographer

- Root word: Electro (o)
  Meaning: Electricity, electric
  Example: Electrolyte – A compound in body fluid that conducts electricity

- Root word:Eosin (o)
  Meaning: Red, rosy
  Example: Eosiniphobia – A morbid fear of the dawn

- Root word: Ergo
  Meaning: Work
  Example: Ergodynamograph – Used to record the degree of muscle force and the amount of work done by muscle contraction

- Root word: Erythro (o)
  Meaning: Red, redness
  Example: Erythrocatalysis – Phagocytosis of RBC

- Root word: Esthesio
  Meaning: Sedation, perception
  Example: Esthesiology – The study of sensory phenomenon

- Root word: Ethmo
  Meaning: Ethmoid bone
  Example: Ethmoiditis – Inflammation of the ethmoid sinuses

- Root word: Etio
  Meaning: Cause
  Example: Etiology – The study of the cause of diseases and their mode of operation

- Root word: Fibr (o)
  Meaning: Fiber
  Example: Fibroadipose – Relating to or containing both fibrous and fatty structures

- Root word: Fluor (o)
  Meaning: Light, luminous, fluorine
  Example: Fluorocyte – Term used for a reticulocyte that exhibits fluorescence

- Root word: Fungi
  Meaning: Fungus
  Example: Fungitoxic – Poisonous to the growth of fungus

- Root word: Galact (o)
  Meaning: Milk
  Example: Galactocele – Retention of cyst caused by a blocked or narrowing milk duct

- Root word: Gen (o)
  Meaning: Producing, being born
  Example: Genotoxic – A substance that damages DNA and causes in utero mutation or cancer

- Root word: Gero, geront (o)
  Meaning: Old age
  Example: Gerontotherapy – Treatment of disease in the aged

- Root word: Gluco
  Meaning: Glucose
  Example: Glucopenia – low blood sugar

- Root word: Glyco
  Meaning: Sugars
  Example: Glycolipid – A lipid with one or more covalently attached sugar

- Root word: Gonio
  Meaning: Angle
  Example: Gonioscope – A lens designed for the study of the angle of the anterior chamber of the eye

- Root word: Granulo
  Meaning: Granular
  Example: Granuloplastic – forming granules

- Root word: Gyn (o), gyne, gyneco
  Meaning: Women
  Example: Gynecology – The study of genitalia diseases, endocrinology, and reproductive physiology in women

- Root word: Home (o), homo
  Meaning: Same, constant
  Example: Homonuclear – A cell line that retains the original chromosome complement

- Root word: Hydro (o)
  Meaning: Hydrogen, water
  Example: Hydropenia – Reduction or deprivation of water

- Root word: Hypn (o)
  Meaning: Sleep
  Example: Hypnopompic – The occurrence of visions or dreams during a drowsy state following sleep

- Root word: Iatr (o)
  Meaning: Physician, treatment
  Example: Iatrogenic – The response to medical or surgical treatment, usually when response is unfavorable

- Root word: Ichthy (o)
  Meaning: Dry, scaly, fish
  Example: Ichthyism – Poisoning by eating stale fish

- Root word: Idio
  Meaning: Distinct, unknown
  Example: Idiopathic – Of unknown origin

- Root word: Immun (o)
  Meaning: Safe, immune
  Example: Immunosuppressant – An agent that weakens or suppress the immune system

- Root word: Kal (i)
  Meaning: Potassium
  Example: Hypokalemia – Too little potassium present in the blood

- Root word: Karyo
  Meaning: Nucleus
  Example: Karyoplast – A cell nucleus surrounded by a narrow band of cytoplasm and plasma membrane

- Root word: Ket (o), keton (o)
  Meaning: Ketone, acetone
  Example: Ketoacidosis – Acidosis, usually in diabetics or anorexics, caused by enhanced production of ketone bodies

- Root word: Kin (o), kine
  Meaning: Movement
  Example: Kinometer – An instrument used to measure movement

- Root word: Kinesi (o), kineso
  Meaning: Motion
  Example: Kinesthesia – The sense perception of movement

- Root word: Kyph (o)
  Meaning: Humpback
  Example: Kyphoplasty – Injection of bone cement into a compressed vertebra

- Root word: Lact (o), lacti
  Meaning: Milk
  Example: Lactate – To produce milk in the mammary glands

- Root word: Latero
  Meaning: Lateral, to one side
  Example: Laterotrusion – The movement of the jaw bone when chewing

- Root word: Lepto
  Meaning: Light, frail, thin
  Example: Leptocephalous – Having an abnormally tall, narrow cranium

- Root word: Leuk (o)
  Meaning: White
  Example: Leukocytosis – A condition of elevated WBC

- Root word: Lip (o)
  Meaning: Fat
  Example: Liposuction – Removal of unwanted fat by use of a suction cannulae

- Root word: Lith (o)
  Meaning: Stone
  Example: Ureterolithiasis – Formation of one or more calculi in one or both ureters

- Root word: Log (o)
  Meaning : Speech, words, thoughts
  Example: Logopathy – Speech disorder

- Root word: Lys (o)
  Meaning: Dissolution
  Example: Lysis – The destruction of RBC, bacteria, ect. by a specific lysin

- Root word: Macr (o)
  Meaning: Large, long
  Example: Macroscopic – Visible to the naked eye

- Root word: Medi (o)
  Meaning: Middle, medial place
  Example: Mediodorsal – Relating to the median and dorsal planes

- Root word: Meg (a), megal (o)
  Meaning: Large, million
  Example: Megalocardia – Enlarged heart

- Root word: Melan (o)
  Meaning: Black, dark
  Example: Melanuria – Excretion of dark colored urine

- Root word: Mes (o)
  Meaning: Middle, median
  Example: Mesocardia – Atypical location of the heart in the central thorax

- Root word: Micr (o)
  Meaning: Small, one-millionth, tiny
  Example: Microscopic – Visible only with the aid of a microscope; of minute size.

- Root word: Mio
  Meaning: Smaller, less
  Example: Miosis – Contraction of the pupil

- Root word: Morph (o)
  Meaning: Structure, shape
  Example: Morphosis – Mode of development of a part

- Root word: Narco
  Meaning: Sleep, numbness
  Example: Narcolepsy – Sleep disorder causing frequent day sleep and interrupted night sleep

- Root word: Necr (o)
  Meaning: Death, dying
  Example: Necrosis – Pathological death of one or more cells, tissue, or organs with irreversible changes

- Root word: Noct (i)
  Meaning: Night
  Example: Nocturnal – pertaining to the hours of darkness

- Root word: Norm (o)
  Meaning: Normal
  Example: Normobaric – The barometric pressure equivalent to the pressure at sea level

- Root word: Nucle
  Meaning: Nucleus
  Example: Nucleon – One of the subatomic partials of anomic partials, ex. Proton

- Root word: Nyct (o)
  Meaning: Night
  Example: Nyctophobia – Morbid fear of night time or darkness

- Root word: Oncho, onco
  Meaning: Tumor
  Example: Oncology – The study of neoplastic growths

- Root word: Orth (o)
  Meaning: Straight, normal
  Example: Orthodontics – Dental specialty concerned with the correction of tooth placement

- Root word: Oxy
  Meaning: Sharp, acute, oxygen
  Example: Oxyphonia – Shrill or high pitch of the voice

- Root word: Pachy
  Meaning: Thick
  Example: Pachyblepharon – Thickening of the tarsal boarder of the eyelid

- Root word: Path (o)
  Meaning: Disease
  Example: Pathogen – Disease causing substance

- Root word: Phago
  Meaning: Eating, devouring, swallowing
  Example: Phagocyte – A cell that ingests bacteria and other intruders

- Root word: Pharmaco
  Meaning: Drugs, medicine
  Example: Pharmacology – The study of drugs

- Root word: Phon (o)
  Meaning: Sound, voice, speech
  Example: Phonetics – The science of speech and pronunciation

- Root word: Phot (o)
  Meaning: Light
  Example: Photogen – A microorganism that produced luminescence

- Root word: Physic, physio
  Meaning: Physical, natural
  Example: Physiotherapeutic – Pertaining to physical therapy

- Root word: Physo
  Meaning: Air, gas, growing
  Example: Physocele – Herniated sac distended with gas

- Root word: Phyt (o)
  Meaning: Plant
  Example: Phytodermatitis – Dermatitis caused by skin contacting and reacting to specific plants

- Root word: Plasma, plasmo
  Meaning: Formative, plasma
  Example: Plasmoschisis – The splitting of protoplasm into fragments

- Root wrd: Poikilo
  Meaning: Varied, irregular
  Example: Poikiloblast – A nucleated RBC of irregular shape

- Root word: Pseud (o)
  Meaning: False
  Example: Pseudoapraxia – A condition of exaggerated awkwardness in which an individual make wrong use of objects

- Root word: Pyo
  Meaning: Pus
  Example: Pyuria – Pus in the urine

- Root word: Pyreto
  Meaning: Fever
  Example: Pyretogenesis – The origin of a fever

- Root word: Pyro
  Meaning: Fever, fire, heat
  Example: Pyrolysis – Decomposition of a substance by heat

- Root word: Radio
  Meaning: Radiation, x-ray, radius
  Example: Radiologist – A physician trained in diagnostic / therapeutic use of x-ray and radionuclides

- Root word: Salping (o)
  Meaning: Tube
  Example: Salpingoophorectomy – Removal of the ovary and itâ€™s uterine tube

- Root word: Schisto
  Meaning: Split
  Example: Schisocelia – Congenital fissure of the abdominal wall

- Root word: Schiz (o)
  Meaning: Split, division
  Example: Schizotonia – Division of the distribution of tone in the muscle

- Root word: Scler (o)
  Meaning: Hardness, hardening
  Example: Scleroblastema – The embryonic tissue entering into the formation of bone

- Root word: Scolio
  Meaning; Cooked, bent
  Example: Scoliosis – Condition of abnormal lateral and rotational spine curvature

- Root word: Scoto
  Meaning: Darkness
  Example: Scotopic – Referring to low illumination in which the eye is dark adapted

- Root word: Sidero
  Meaning: Iron
  Example: Siderocyte – An erythrocyte containing granules of free iron

- Root word: Sito
  Meaning: Food, grain
  Example: Sitosterol – A plant-derived chemical similar to cholesterol, commonly found in wheat germ, soy beans, and corn oil.

- Root word: Somat (o)
  Meaning: Body
  Example: Somatalgia – Pain in the body

- Root word: Sono
  Meaning: Sound
  Example: Ultrasonography – containing few or no echoes of sound waves

- Root word: Spasmo
  Meaning: Spasm
  Example: Spasmogen – A substance causing a smooth muscle to contract

- Root word: Sphere (o)
  Meaning: Round, spherical
  Example: Sphereocytosis – The presence of sheric RBCs in the blood

- Root word; Spir (o)
  Meaning: Breath, breathe
  Example: Spiroscope – A device for measuring air capacity in the lungs

- Root word: Squamo
  Meaning: Scale, squamous
  Example: Squamocellular – Relating to or having squamous epithelium

- Root word: Staphyl (o)
  Meaning: Grapelike cluster
  Example:Staphylococcus – Common species that is the cause of a variety of infections

- Root word: Steno
  Meaning: Narrowness
  Example: Stenosis – A narrowing or stricture of any canal or orifice

- Root word: Stere (o)
  Meaning: Three-dimensional
  Example: Stereology – A study of three-dimensional aspects of a cell or microscopic structure

- Root word: Strepto
  Meaning: Twisted chains, streptococci
  Example: Streptococcus – A common organism that causes various infections

- Root word: Styl (o)
  Meaning: Peg-shaped
  Example: Stylomastoid – Relating to the styloid and mastoid processes of the temporal bone

- Root word: Syring (o)
  Meaning:
  Example: Syringe – An instrument used for injecting or withdrawing fluid

- Root word: Tel (o), tele (o)
  Meaning: Distant, end, complete
  Example: Teletherapy – Radiation treatment administered with the source at a distance from the body

- Root word: Terato
  Meaning: Monster (as in malformed fetus)
  Example: Teratogen – An agent that causes a malformed fetus

- Root word: Therm (o)
  Meaning: Heat
  Example: Thermometer – An instrument used to measure temperature

- Root word: Tono
  Meaning: Tension, pressure
  Example: Tonometry – Measurement of tension ex. Blood pressure

- Root word: Top (o)
  Meaning: Place, topical
  Example: Topophobia – A neurotic dread of a particular place

- Root word:Tox (i), toxico, toxo
  Meaning: Poison, toxin
  Example: Toxicoid – Having an action like that of a poison

- Root word: Tropho
  Meaning: Food, nutrition
  Example: Trophodynamics – The dynamics of nutrition or the metabolism (nutritional energy)

- Root word: Vivi
  Meaning: Life
  Example: Vivisection – Any cutting operation on a living animal for purposes of experimentation

- Root word: Xanth (o)
  Meaning: Yellow
  Example: Xanthoma – A yellow nodule or plaque

- Root word: Xeno
  Meaning: Stranger
  Example: Xenograft – A graft transfer from one species to another

- Root word: Xer (o)
  Meaning: Dry
  Example: Xerochilia – Dryness of the lips

- Root word: Xiph (o)
  Meaning: Sword, xiphoid
  Example: Xiphopagus – Conjoined twins united in the region of the xiphoid process
- Root word: Zo (o)
  Meaning: Life
  Example: Zoograft – A graft from an animal to a human
- Root word: Zym (o)
  Meaning: Fermentation, enzyme
  Example: Zygote – Diploid cell resulting from the union of a sperm and a secondary oocyte

Medical Terminology: Suffixes

- Suffix: –ad
  Meaning: Toward
  Example: Cephalad – toward the head

- Suffix: –algia
  Meaning: Pain
  Example: Cervicalgia – neck pain

- Suffix: –asthenia
  Meaning: Weakness
  Example: Myasthenia – muscle weakness

- Suffix: –blast
  Meaning: Immature, forming
  Example: Cytoblast – immature cell

- Suffix: –cele
  Meaning: Hernia
  Example: Hydrocele – a collection of serous fluid in a sacculated cavity

- Suffix: –cidal, –cide
  Meaning: Destroying, killing
  Example: Cytocide – an agent that is destructive to cells

- Suffix: –clasis
  Meaning:
  Breaking Example: Osteoclasis – intentional breaking of the bone

- Suffix: –clast
  Meaning: Breaking instrument
  Example: Cranioclast – an obsolete instrument used for crushing the head of a demised fetus for extraction

- Suffix: –crine
  Meaning: Secreting
  Example: Apocrine – gland that secretes hormones

- Suffix: –crit
  Meaning: Separate
  Example: Hematocrit – percentage of volume of blood sample that is composed of cells

- Suffix: –cyte
  Meaning: Cell
  Example: Leukocyte – white blood cell

- Suffix: –cytosis
  Meaning: Condition of cells
  Example: Leukocytosis – condition of elevated white blood cells

- Suffix: –derma
  Meaning: Skin
  Example: Leukoderma – an absence of pigment in the skin

- Suffix: –desis
  Meaning: Binding
  Example: Pleurodesis – a fibrous adheasion between two layers of pleura

- Suffix: –dynia
  Meaning: Pain
  Example: Gastrodynia – stomach ache

- Suffix: –ectasia
  Meaning: Expansion, dilation
  Example: Angiectasia – dilation of a lymphatic or blood vessel

- Suffix: –ectomy
  Meaning: Removal of
  Example: Splenectomy – removal of spleen

- Suffix: –edema
  Meaning: Swelling
  Example: Myxedema – hypothyroid charecterized by a hard swelling of subcutaneous tissue

- Suffix: –ema
  Meaning: Condition
  Example: Emphysema – a condition of the lungs involving enlarged air space in connective tissue

- Suffix: –emesis
  Meaning: Vomiting
  Example: Hyperemesis – excessive vomiting

- Suffix: – emia
  Meaning: Blood
  Example: Hypokalemia – abnormal low potassium in the blood

- Suffix: –emic
  Meaning: Relating to blood
  Example: Hyperemic – denoting increased blood flow to a part or organ

- Suffix: –esthesia
  Meaning: Sensation
  Example: Parasthesia – abnormal sensation, such a tingling

- Suffix: –form
  Meaning: In the shape of
  Example: Chloroform – used as an inhalent to produce general anesthesia

- Suffix: –gen
  Meaning: A substance or agent producing, coming to be
  Example: Oxygen – gaseous element essential to plant and animal life

- Suffix: –genesis
  Meaning: Production of
  Example: Osteogenesis – the production of bone

- Suffix: –genic
  Meaning: Producing
  Example: Cytogenic – forming or producing of cells

- Suffix: –globin
  Meaning: Protein
  Example: Hemaglobin – protein of red blood cells

- Suffix: –globulin
  Meaning: Protein
  Example: Gamma-globulin – a protiet in the blood, ie. immunoglobulin

- Suffix: –gram
  Meaning: A recording
  Example: Arthrogram – imaging of a joint by contrast material

- Suffix: –graph
  Meaning: Recording instrument
  Example: Cardiograph – an instrument for graphically recordingmovements of the heart

- Suffix: –graphy
  Meaning: Process of recording
  Example: Angiography – radiography of blood vessles by contrast agent

- Suffix: –iasis
  Meaning: Pathological condition or state
  Example: Cholelithasis – pressence of stone in the gallbladder

- Suffix: –ic
  Meaning: Pertaining to
  Example: Anemic – pertaining to the blood

- Suffix: –ics
  Meaning: Treatment, practice, body of knowledge
  Example – Pediatric – a medical practice concerned with treatment of children

- Suffix: –ism
  Meaning: Condition, disease, doctrine
  Example: Hypothyroidism – the condition of having an abnormally low producing thyroid

- Suffix: –itis
  Meaning: Inflammation
  Example: Dermatitis – an inflammation of the skin

- Suffix: –kinesia; –kinesis
  Meaning: Movement
  Example: Hyperkinesis – excessive muscular movement

- Suffix: –lepsy
  Meaning: Condition of
  Example: Epilepsy – condition with having seizures

- Suffix: –leptic
  Meaning: Having seizures
  Example: Epileptic – person with epilepsy

- Suffix: –logist
  Meaning: One who practices
  Example: Cartiologist – one who practices medicine of the heart

- Suffix: –logy
  Meaning: Study, practice
  Example: Pathology – study of diseases

- Suffix: –lysis
  Meaning: Destruction of
  Example: Paralysis – loss of power of voluntary movement

- Suffix: -lytic
  Meaning: Destroying
  Example: Hemolytic - agent that is destructive to blood cells

- Suffix: -malacia
  Meaning: Softening
  Example: Osteomalacia - gradual softening of bone

- Suffix: -mania
  Meaning: Obsession
  Example: Pyromania - obsessive thoughts regarding fire

- Suffix: -megaly
  Meaning: Enlargement
  Example: Cardiomegaly - abnormal enlargement of the heart

- Suffix: -meter
  Meaning: Measuring device
  Examle: Thermometer - used for measuring temperature

- Suffix: -metry
  Meaning: Measurement
  Example: Oximetry - device used to measure oxygen saturation

- Suffix: -oid
  Meaning: Like, resembling
  Example: Hemorrhoid - varicose condition of the external hemorrhoidal vein

- Suffix: -oma
  Meaning: Tumor, neoplasm
  Example: Glioma - neoplasm of the brain

- Suffix: -opia; -opsia
  Meaning: Vision
  Example: Diplopia - double vision

- Suffix: -opsy
  Meaning: View of
  Example: Autopsy - examination of a dead body's organs

- Suffix: -osis
  Meaning: Condition, state, process
  Example: Keratosis - any lesion on the skin marked by overgrowths from the horny layer

- Suffix: -ostomy
  Meaning: Opening
  Example: Tracheostomy - surgical opening in the trachea

- Suffix: -oxia
  Meaning: Oxygen
  Example: Hypoxia - abnormally low levels of oxygen prior to anoxia

- Suffix: -para
  Meaning: Bearing
  Example: Primipara - woman who has given birth once

- Suffix: -paresis
  Meaning: Slight paralysis
  Example: Hemiparesis - weakness effecting one side of the body

- Suffix: -parous
  Meaning: Producing, bearing
  Meaning: Gemmiparous - reproducing by buds

- Suffix: -pathy
  Meaning: Disease
  Example: Cardiopathy - any disease of the heart

- Suffix: -penia
  Meaning: Deficiency
  Example: Thrombocytopenia - condition of low numbers of thrombocytes in the blood

- Suffix: -pepsia
  Meaning: Digestion
  Example: Hyperpepsia - abnormally rapid digestion

- Suffix: -pexy
  Meaning: Fixation, usually done surgically
  Example: Hysteropexy - fixation of a displaced uterus

- Suffix: -phage; -phagia; -phagy
  Meaning: Eating, devouring
  Example: Macrophage - a cell that eats invaders

- Suffix: -phasia
  Meaning: Speaking
  Example: Dyshasia - difficulty in swallowing

- Suffix: -pheresis
  Meaning: Removal
  Example: Leukapheresis - removal of leukocytes from drawn blood

- Suffix: -phil; -philia
  Meaning: Attraction, affinity for
  Example: Hemephilia - permenant tendencey toward bleeding

- Suffix: -phobia
  Meaning: Fear
  Example: Agoraphobia - irrational fear of the open or unfamiliar

- Suffix: -phonia
  Meaning: Sound
  Example: Dysphonia - altered voice production

- Suffix: -phoresis
  Meaning: Carrying
  Example: Diaphoresis - perspiration

- Suffix: -phoria
  Meaning: Feeling, carrying
  Example: Adiphoria - non-response to stimuli

- Suffix: -phrenia
  Meaning: Of the mind
  Example: Hebephrenia - a disorganized type of schizophrenia

- Suffix: -phthisis
  Meaning: Wasting away
  Example: Hemophthisis - anemia

- Suffix: -phylaxis
  Meaning: Protection
  Example: Anaphylaxis – a severe reaction to an agent the body recognizes as an invader

- Suffix: -physis
  Meaning: Growing
  Example: Epiphysis – part of a long bone distinct from and growing out of the shaft

- Suffix: -plakia
  Meaning: Plaque
  Example: melanoplakia – colored patches on the mucous membrane

- Suffix: -plasia
  Meaning: Formation
  Example: Hyperplasia – an increase of the normal number of cells in an organ

- Suffix: -plasm
  Meaning: Formation
  Example: Cytoplasm – a substance of protoplasm in a cell

- Suffix: -plastic
  Meaning: Forming
  Example: Neoplastic – containing a neoplasm or the charecteristics of one

- Suffix: -plasty
  Meaning: Surgical repair
  Example: Dermaplasty – surgical repair of the skin

- Suffix: -plegia
  Meaning: Paralysis
  Example: Paraplegia – paralysis of both lother extremities

- Suffix: -plegic
  Meaning: One who is paralyzed
  Example: Paraplegic – one who has pariplegia

- Suffix: -pnea
  Meaning: Breath
  Example: Dyspnea – difficult or abnormal breathing

- Suffix: -poiesis
  Meaning: Formation
  Example: Thrombopoiesis – formation of thrombocytes

- Suffix: -poietic
  Meaning: Forming
  Example: Erythropoietic – of the formation of red blood cells

- Suffix: -poietin
  Meaning: One that forms
  Example: Erythropoietin – an acid that aids in the formation of red blood cells

- Suffix: -porosis
  Meaning: Lessening in density
  Example: Osteoporosis – lessening if bone density

- Suffix: -ptosis
  Meaning: Falling down, drooping
  Example: Nephroptosis – when the kidney sinks into the pelvis cavity

- Suffix: -rrhage
  Meaning: Discharging heavily
  Example: Hemorhhage – to bleed heavily

- Suffix: -rrhagia
  Meaning: Heavy discharge Example: Menorrhagia – Excessive mestrual bleeding

- Suffix: -rrhaphy
  Meaning: Surgical suturing
  Example: Colorrhaphy – suture of the colon

- Suffix: -rrhea
  Meaning: A flowing, a flux
  Example: Rhinorrhea – runny nose

- Suffix: -rrhexis
  Meaning: Rupture
  Example: Angiorrhexis – ruptured blood vessel

- Suffix: -schisis
  Meaning: Splitting internal body cavity
  Example: Spondyloschisis – failure of fusion of the vertebral arch in an embryo

- Suffix: -scope
  Meaning: Instrument (especially one used for observing)
  Example: Laparoscope – a scope used for examining the peritoneal cavity

- Suffix: -scopy
  Meaning; Use of an instrument for observing
  Example: Endoscopy – use of instruments to view an

- Suffix: -somnia
  Meaning: Sleep
  Example: Hypersomnia – excessive day time sleep

- Suffix: -spasm
  Meaning: Contraction
  Example: Myospasm – spasmotic contractions of the muscle

- Suffix: -stalsis
  Meaning: Contraction
  Example: Retrostalsis – backward motion of the intestine

- Suffix: -stasis
  Meaning: Stopping, constant
  Example: Cholestasis – a condition where bile flow from the liver is blocked

- Suffix: -stat
  Meaning: Agent to maintain a state
  Example: Hemostat – an agent that arrests the blow of blood

- Suffix: -static
  Meaning: Maintaining a state
  Example: Orthostatic – relating to an erect posture

- Suffix: -stenosis
  Meaning: Narrowing
  Example: Aortic stenosis – a narrowing of the aortic valve

- Suffix: –stomy
  Meaning: Opening
  Example: Gastrostomy – surgical opening in the stomach (usually for a feeding tube)

- Suffix: –tome
  Meaning: Cutting instrument, segment
  Example: Dermatome – an instrument for making thin slices of the skin

- Suffix: –tomy
  Meaning: Cutting operation
  Example: Craniotomy – surgical operation that removes a portion of the skull to acess the brain

- Suffix: –trophic
  Meaning: Nutritional
  Example: Hypotrophic – progressive degeneration of organs and tissue

- Suffix: –trophy
  Meaning: Nutrition
  Example: Atrophy – a wasting away of the body

- Suffix: –tropia
  Meaning: Turning
  Example: Anatropia – deviation of the axis of one eye upward

- Suffix: –tropic
  Meaning: Turning toward
  Example: Dexiotropic – twisting in a spiral fashion from left to right

- Suffix: –tropy
  Meaning: Condition of turning toward
  Example: Neurotropy – affinity of certain contrasts mediums for nervous tissue

- Suffix: –uria
  Meaning: Urine
  Example: Dysuria – painful or difficult urination

- Suffix: –version
  Meaning: Turning
  Example: Retroversion – a turning backward

Proctor – to – Coder Instructions
To Be Read to Examinees

1. Welcome to the AAPC Certification Coding Exam. My name is **[state your name]** and this is **[state second proctor's name.]** We are the proctors for your examination today.

2. Each of you has been given a copy of the Proctor-To- Coder Instructions along with an exam packet. Your exam packet contains a test grid, marking instructions for grid, gold seals and exam booklet. Please open only your exam packet saving the white adhesive label on the plastic shrink-wrap. Set aside the gold seals, and verify you have the correct type of examination booklet for the exam you are taking (CPC®, CPC-H®, CPC-P®, CIRCC®, CPMA®, or Specialty) and then set it aside with the gold seals (do not break the silver seals on your exam booklet yet.)

   Locate the Important Grid Marking Instruction form. Please read carefully, and using a #2 pencil complete form. Once the form is completed it will be collected prior to beginning the exam. If there are any questions regarding how to fill out the grid correctly please inquire now.

3. Using a #2 pencil, please fill out sections A, B and C of the examination answer grid at this time. For Section B, the Index Number is located on the white adhesive label of your exam packet. Please make sure you are filling in each bubble on your test grid completely, reference the upper right hand corner of the test grid for an example.

4. Now complete Section D of the test grid. Please refer to the back of the exam booklet for the exam type, version and exam number. For assistance with your member ID# refer to the white adhesive label, which is located on the exam plastic.

5. The exam length is 5 hours and 40 minutes. Eating or drinking is permitted during the exam, but make sure examination grids remain dry and clean. Breaks are allowed (as needed) during the exam; however the exam clock **will not stop** when an examinee elects to take a break. Only one examinee may take a break and leave the examination room at a time. Removal of any test material from the exam site is strictly prohibited. Any attempt to remove exam materials will disqualify the examinee for certification and result in automatic failure of the examination.

6. Because this is a timed test, there is no requirement for the examination to be completed in a particular order. It is recommended that you complete all questions that require more time. AAPC does advise that examinees should not leave any questions unanswered. You will be notified when 30 minutes of test time is remaining.

7. Upon completion of your exam, locate your gold seals and put them on the top, right side and bottom of your exam booklet (but **do NOT** seal your test grid in the booklet.) Fill out sections F and G on the answer grid and return your exam booklet, test grid (and E/M Audit Sheets, if applicable) to us before exiting the room. If you finish your exam before the 5 hours and 40 minutes are up, you may leave. When exiting the exam room, please be quiet and courteous of other test takers.

8. Any collaborative or disruptive behavior detected during the examination is cause for immediate action (disqualification, etc.) by the proctors. Electronic devices capable of storing and retrieving text, audio books, etc. may not be brought into the examination room. Please turn off and put away all cell phones and/or pagers. Examination content is confidential, therefore, copying questions and/or discussing the questions with others during or following the examination will disqualify you from certification. Removal of any test material from the exam site is strictly prohibited. Any attempt to remove exam materials will disqualify the examinee for certification and result in automatic failure of the examination. Proctors may not clarify test questions during the examination.

9. If at **ANY TIME** during the exam you are distracted because of the exam environment, you may elect to stop taking the exam. The exam will not be graded, your attempt will not be counted and you will need to contact the AAPC to reschedule your exam at a later date.

10. Exam results are usually released within 5 to 7 business days after AAPC receives the exam package back from the proctor. Results will be accessible in your member area on the AAPC web site (www.aapc.com) and official result documents will be mailed within 2 weeks of their receipt at the national office. **Please do not call AAPC for your test results. Exam results are prohibited from being released over the telephone.** We are now ready to begin the examination, you make break the silver seals and open your test booklet. **Use only a #2 pencil to mark your answers and please correctly bubble in each answer on your test grid.** You have 5 hours and 40 minutes to complete the examination, the current time is **[state the time.]** The exam will end at **[state the time.]**

150 Question Medical Coding Exam

Medical Terminology

1. The suffix -ectomy means
   a. Cutting into
   b. Surgical removal
   c. A permanent opening
   d. Surgical repair

2. The acronym MMRV stands for
   a. Measles, Mumps, and Rubella vaccine
   b. Measles, Mumps, and Rosella vaccine
   c. Measles, Mumps, Rubella, and Varicella
   d. Measles, Mumps, Rosella, and Varicella

3. MRI stands for
   a. Micro-wave Recording Instrument
   b. Medical Recording Instrument
   c. Magnetic Resolution Image
   d. Magnetic Resonance Imaging

4. The term "Salpingo-Oophorectomy" refers to
   a. The removal of the fallopian tubes and ovaries
   b. The surgical sampling or removal of a fertilized egg
   c. Cutting into the fallopian tubes and ovaries for surgical purposes
   d. Cutting into a fertilized egg for surgical purposes

5. PERRLA stands for what?
   a. Pupils Equivalent, Rapid in Response to Light and Accommodation
   b. Pupil Equal, Rapid in Response to Light and Accommodation
   c. Pupil Equivalent, Round, Reactive to Light and Accommodation
   d. Pupils Equal, Round, Reactive to Light and Accommodation

6. Cryopreservation is a means of preserving something through
   a. Saturation
   b. Heat
   c. Freezing
   d. Chemicals

7. Which of the following describes the removal of fluid from a body cavity
    a. Arthrocentesis
    b. Amniocentesis
    c. Pericardiocentesis
    d. Paracentesis

8. If a surgeon cuts into a patient's stomach he has performed a
    a. Gastrectomy
    b. Gastrotomy
    c. Gastrostomy
    d. Gastrorrhaphy

9. The terms Nephro and Renal both refer to the same organ
    a. True
    b. False

10. In the medical term myopathy the term pathy means disease. What is diseased?
    a. Mind
    b. Muscle
    c. Eye
    d. Nervous System

Anatomy

11. The Radius is the
    a. Outer bone located in the forearm
    b. Outer bone located in the lower leg
    c. Inner bone located in the forearm
    d. Inner bone located in the lower leg

12. The spleen belongs to what organ system?
    a. Endocrine
    b. Hemic and Lymphatic
    c. Digestive
    d. Nervous

13. The portion of the femur bone that helps makes up the knee cap is considered what?
    a. The posterior portion
    b. The proximal portion
    c. The distal portion
    d. The dorsal portion

14. How many regions are in the abdominopelvic cavity?
    a. Four
    b. Six
    c. Eight
    d. Nine

15. The Midsagittal plane refers to what portion of the body?
    a. Top
    b. Middle
    c. Bottom
    d. Back

16. Which of the following is not part of the small intestine?
    a. Duodenum
    b. Ileum
    c. Jejunum
    d. Cecum

17. The round window is located in the
    a. Pericardium
    b. Anterior aqueous chamber of the eye
    c. Inner ear
    d. Middle ear

18. The point of an organ or body part nearest the point of attachments is
    a. Distal
    b. Proximal
    c. Lateral
    d. Medial

19. One of the six major scapulohumeral muscles
    a. Temporalis
    b. Trapezius
    c. Teres
    d. Trigone

20. The cardia fundus is
    a. Part of the heart wall that causes contractions
    b. Where to esophagus joins the stomach
    c. A fungal infection that attacks the heart
    d. Part of the female reproductive system

Coding Concepts

21. CPT codes 22840-22848 are modifier 62 exempt?
    a. True
    b. False

22. An ABN must be signed when?
    a. Once the insurance company has denied payment
    b. Before the service or procedure is provided to the patient
    c. After services are rendered, but before the claim is filed
    d. Once the denied claim has been appealed at the highest level

23. Wound exploration codes include the following service (s):
    a. Exploration and repair
    b. Exploration, including enlargement, removal of foreign body (-ies), repair
    c. Exploration, including enlargement, repair, and necessary grafting
    d. Exploration, including enlargement, debridement, removal of foreign body (-ies), minor vessel ligation, and repair

24. The full description of CPT code 24925 is:
    a. Secondary closure or scar revision
    b. Amputation, secondary closure or scar revision
    c. Amputation, arm through humerus; secondary closure or scar revision
    d. Amputation, arm through humerus; with primary closure, secondary closure or scar revision

25. Medical necessity means what?
    a. Without treatment the patient will suffer permanent disability or death
    b. The service requires medical treatment
    c. The condition of the patient justifies the service provided
    d. The care provided met quality standards

26. The following statement does not apply to what code type: These codes are never stand-alone codes and never primary codes.
    a. E codes
    b. Add on codes
    c. Late effect codes
    d. V codes

27. Which of the following codes allows the use of modifier 51?
    a. 20975
    b. 93600
    c. 31500
    d. 45392

28. Category III codes are temporary codes for emerging technology, services, and procedures. If a category III code exists it should be used instead of an "unlisted procedure" code in category I (example of an unlisted category I code: 60699).
    a. True
    b. False

29. Which of the following statements is not true regarding Medicare Part A
    a. It helps cover home health care charges
    b. It helps cover skilled nursing facility charges
    c. It helps cover hospice charges
    d. It helps cover outpatient charges

30. Which of the following is not one of the three components of HIPAA that is enforced by the office for civil rights?
    a. Protecting the privacy of individually identifiable health information
    b. Setting national standards for the security of electronic protected health information
    c. Protecting identifiable information being used to analyze patient safety events and improve patient safety
    d. Setting national standards regarding the transmission and use of protected health information

31. What is the correct ICD-9-CM code(s) for malignant hypertension with stage III kidney disease?
    a. 401.0, 585.3
    b. 403.00
    c. 401.0
    d. 403.00, 585.3

32. Lucy was standing on a chair in her kitchen trying to change a light bulb when she slipped and fell. She struck the glass top stove, which shattered. She presents to the ER with a simple laceration to her forearm that has embedded glass particles.
    a. 881.00, E888.0, E849.0
    b. 881.10, E888.0, E920.8
    c. 881.00, E888.1, E849.0
    d. 881.10, E888.1, E920.8

33. Jim was at a bonfire when he tripped and fell into the flames. Jim sustained multiple burns. He came to the emergency room via an ambulance and was treated for second and third degree burns on his face, second-degree burn on his shoulders and forearms, and third degree burns on the fronts of his thighs.
    a. 941.20, 841.30, 943.25, 943.21, 945.36, 948.42, E897
    b. 941.30, 943.29, 945.36, 948.42, E897
    c. 941.09, 943.09, 945.09, 948.64, E897
    d. 941.30, 943.29, 945.36, 948.64, E897

34. A 35-year-old woman who is pregnant with her first child is admitted to the hospital. She experiences a prolonged labor during the first stage and eventually births a healthy baby boy.
    a. 662.00, 659.6, V27.0
    b. 650, V27.0
    c. 650, 662.01, 659.6, V27.0
    d. 662.01, 659.5, V27.0

35. Henry was playing baseball and slid for home base where he collided with another player. He presents to the emergency department complaining of pain in the distal portion of his right middle finger. It is swollen and deformed. The physician orders an x-ray and diagnoses Henry with a tuft fracture. He splints the finger, provides narcotics for pain, and instructs Henry to follow-up with his orthopedist in two weeks.
    a. 816.02, E007.3
    b. 815.03, E917.0

c. 814.09, E007.3
d. 815.04, E917.0

36. A 60-year-old male is admitted for detoxification and rehabilitation. He has continuously abused amphetamines to the point that he cannot voluntarily stop on his own and has become dependent upon them. He also has a long documented history of alcohol abuse and alcoholism. He experiences high levels of anxiety due to PTSD, which causes him to use and abuse substances.
    a. 305.71, 304.41, 305.00, 303.91, 300.02, 309.81
    b. 304.41, 303.91, 300.00, 309.81
    c. 304.71, 305.00, 300.00, 309.81
    d. 305.71, 304.41, 305.00, 303.91, 300.00, 309.81

37. A patient with uncontrolled type II diabetes is experiencing blurred vision and an increase in floaters appearing in her vision. She is diagnosed with diabetic retinopathy.
    a. 250.00, 362.0
    b. 362.01, 250.52
    c. 250.52, 362.01
    d. 362.10, 250.02

38. Signs and symptoms that are associated routinely with a disease process should not be assigned as additional codes, unless otherwise instructed by classification.
    a. True
    b. False

39. A patient who is known to be HIV positive but who has no documented symptoms would be assigned code
    a. 042
    b. 795.71
    c. V08
    d. 079.53

40. A patient fell asleep on the beach and comes in with blistering on her back. She is diagnosed with second-degree solar radiation burns.
    a. 692.76
    b. 692.72
    c. 942.24
    d. 692.82

HCPCS

41. A patient has a home health aide come to his home to clean and dress a burn on his lower leg. The aide uses a special absorptive, sterile dressing to cover a 20 sq. cm. area. She also covers a 15sq. cm. area with a self-adhesive sterile gauze pad.
    a. A6204, A6403
    b. A6252, A6403
    c. A6252, A6219
    d. A6204, A6219

42. A 12-year-old arrives in his pediatrician's office after colliding with another player during a soccer game. He is complaining of pain in his right wrist. The physician orders an x-ray and diagnoses him with a hairline fracture of the distal radius. He has a short arm fiberglass cast applied and discharges him with follow up instructions.
    a. Q4009
    b. Q4012
    c. Q4022
    d. Q4010

43. A patient with Hodgkin's disease takes Neosar as part of his chemotherapy regiment. He receives 100 mg once a week through intravenous infusion.
    a. J9100
    b. J7502
    c. J9070
    d. J8999

44. A patient with diabetes is fitted for custom molded shoes. What is the code range for such a fitting?
    a. L3201-L3649
    b. A5500-A5513
    c. K0001-K0899
    d. E0100-E8002

45. A 300 lb. paraplegic needs a special sized wheelchair with fixed arm rests and elevating leg rests.
    a. E1195
    b. E1222
    c. E1160
    d. E1087

46. A patient comes into her doctor's office for her weekly blood sugar check. The LPN on staff draws her blood; the visit takes about 5 minutes total.
    a. 99201
    b. 99212
    c. 99211
    d. 99363

47. A three-year-old child is brought into the ER after swallowing a penny. A detailed history and exam are taken on the child and medical decision-making is of moderate complexity. The child is admitted to observation for three hours and is then discharged home.
    a. 99218
    b. 99235
    c. 99218; 99217
    d. 99234

48. A 20-month-old child is admitted to the hospital with pneumonia and acute respiratory distress. The physician spends 3 minutes intubating the child and spends 90 minutes of Critical Care time stabilizing the patient.
    a. 99291; 99292-25; 31500; 518.82; 486
    b. 99471-25; 31500; 786.09; 486
    c. 99291-25; 99292-25; 31500; 786.09; 486
    d. 99471; 518.82; 486

49. At the request of a physician who is delivering for a high-risk pregnancy, Dr. Smith, a pediatrician, is present in the delivery room to assist the infant if needed. After thirty minutes the infant is born, but is not breathing. The delivering physician hands the infant to Dr. Smith who provides chest compressions and resuscitates the infant. The pediatrician then performs the initial evaluation and management and admits the healthy newborn to the nursery. What codes should Dr. Smith submit on a claim?
    a. 99360; 99465
    b. 99465; 99460
    c. 99360; 99460
    d. 99360; 99465; 99460

50. Mr. Johnson is a 79-year-old established male patient that is seen by Dr. Anderson for his annual physical exam. During the examination Dr. Anderson notices a suspicious mole on Mr. Johnson's back. The Doctor completes the annual exam and documents a detailed history and exam and the time discussing the patient's need to quit smoking. Dr. Anderson then turns his attention to the mole and does a complete work up. He documents a comprehensive history and examination and medical decision making of moderate complexity. He also called a local dermatologist and made an appointment for Mr. Johnson to see him the next day for an evaluation and biopsy.
    a. 99387, 99205
    b. 99387, 99215
    c. 99397, 99205
    d. 99397, 99215

51. An E/M is made up of seven components six of which are used in defining the levels of E/M services. The seven components include History, Exam, Medical Decision Making, Counseling, Coordination of Care, Nature of Presenting Problem, and Time. Which six of these seven parts help define the level of the E/M service?
    a. History, Exam, Medical Decision Making, Coordination of Care, Nature of Presenting Problem, and Time
    b. History, Exam, Medical Decision Making, Counseling, Nature of Presenting Problem, and Time
    c. History, Exam, Medical Decision Making, Counseling, Coordination of Care, and Nature of Presenting Problem
    d. History, Exam, Medical Decision Making, Counseling, Coordination of Care, and Time

52. The correct anesthesia code for a ventral hernia repair on a 13 month old child is
    a. 00830
    b. 00834
    c. 00832
    d. 00820

53. A patient is placed under anesthesia to have an exploratory surgery done on her wrist. The surgeon utilizes a small fiber optic scope and investigates the radius, ulna, and surrounding wrist bones. What should the anesthesiologist code for?
    a. 01829
    b. 01820
    c. 01830
    d. 29840

54. When does anesthesia time begin?
    a. After the induction of anesthesia is complete
    b. During the pre-operative exam prior to entering the OR
    c. When the anesthesiologist begins preparing the patient for the induction of anesthesia
    d. Once the supervising physician signs over the patient's care to the anesthesiologist

55. A five month old is brought into the operating room for open heart surgery. The surgeon performs a repair of a small hole that was found in the lining surrounding the patient's heart. Anesthesia was provided as well as the assistance of an oxygenator pump.
    a. 00560, 99100
    b. 00561
    c. 00567, 99100
    d. 00561, 99100

56. A 72-year-old male with a history of severe asthma is placed under anesthesia to have a long tendon in his upper arm repaired
    a. 01712-P4, 99100
    b. 01716-P3
    c. 01714-P3, 99100
    d. 01714-P4

57. Which of the following procedures can be coded separately when performed by the anesthesiologist?
    a. Administration of blood
    b. Monitoring of a central venous line
    c. Capnography
    d. Monitoring of an EKG

58. A female who is 17 weeks pregnant is rushed into the OR due to a ruptured tubal pregnancy. She has a severe hemorrhage and has an emergency laparoscopic tubal ligation.
    a. 00851-P5, 99140
    b. 00880-P4
    c. 01965-P5
    d. 00880-P5, 99140

59. A healthy five-year-old male is placed under anesthesia to have a biopsy taken from his left eardrum.
    a. 00120-P1
    b. 00124-P2
    c. 00170-P2
    d. 00126-P1

60. A 75-year-old healthy male patient sustained a hip dislocation following a fall. He is taken to the OR and plans to be placed under general anesthesia prior to the hip reduction. The anesthesiologist begins preparing the patient at 8:15am. AT 8:30am the patient is induced with anesthesia and the anesthesiologist is monitoring the patient's vitals, ECG, pulse ox, and capnography. The surgeon begins the reduction at 8:45am and completes the procedure at 9:15am. The anesthesiologist monitors the patient until 9:30am when he releases the patient to the nurse for postoperative supervision. At 9:45am the patient is fully alert and taken to recovery. How many minutes of anesthesia time should the anesthesiologist charge for?
    a. 30 minutes
    b. 45 minutes
    c. 1 hour
    d. 1 hour and 15 minutes

61. An 81-year-old female patient with a history of well controlled type two diabetes and a mild history of asthma presents in the operating room for an open reduction with internal fixation for a displaced fracture of the right distal radius.

The patient was laid in the supine position on the operating table. The right arm was prepped and draped in the normal sterile fashion. Prior to the surgery the patient was given 1g of cefazolin intravenously. A tourniquet was place on the upper arm and inflated to 250 mmHg. An incision was made along the dorsal aspect of the forearm and subcutaneous tissue was dissected to reveal the fractured radius. A curette was used to remove the splintered ends of the radius on each side of the fracture and a K-wire was then introduced along the radius to stabilize it. A guide pin was then placed down the central axis of the radius. A 20mm hole was then drilled and a screw was introduced. The K-wire was then removed and the wound was thoroughly irrigated with normal saline. The fascia layer was closed with absorbable sutures and the epidermis was closed with Monocryl. The wound was dressed with Vaseline gauze, 4x4s, and sterile Sof-Rol. A long arm Velcro splint was then placed over this and placed in a sling. The tourniquet was deflated after a total time of 60 minutes. The patient was awakened, placed in his hospital bed, and taken to the recovery room in fair condition.

Estimated blood loss was 15cc. Sponge and needle counts were correct.
   a. 01830-P2, 99100, 813.42, 250.00, 493.90
   b. 10830-P3, 99100, 813.52. 250.00, 493.90
   c. 01810-P2, 99100, 813.42, V12.2, V12.69
   d. 01820-P3, 99100, 813.52, V12.2, V12.69

62. John was in a fight at the local bar and presents to the ER with multiple lacerations. The physician evaluates John and determines that he has a 2.5 cm gash to his left forearm and a 4 cm gash on his right shoulder, both of which require layered closure. He also has a simple 3 cm laceration on his forehead that requires simple closure. What are the correct codes for the laceration repairs?
    a. 12032-RT, 12031-LT, 12013-59, 881.10, 880.10, 873.42
    b. 12032, 12013-59, 881.00, 880.00, 873.42
    c. 13121, 12052-59, 884.1, 873.42
    d. 12032-RT-LT, 12013-59, 881.00, 880.00, 873.42

63. A patient presents to her dermatologists office with three suspicious looking lesions. The dermatologist evaluates them and determines that the 1.3cm lesion of the scalp is benign and the 1.5cm lesion of the neck is premalignant. The 2.5 cm on the dorsal surface of the patient's hand is also evaluated and is determined to be malignant. The dermatologist chooses to ablate all three lesions using electrosurgery.
    a. 17273, 17003, 17110
    b. 17273, 17000, 17003
    c. 17273, 17000, 17110
    d. 17273, 17003

64. An 18-year-old female presents with a cyst of her left breast and her physician performs a puncture aspiration.
    a. 10160
    b. 10060
    c. 10021
    d. 19000

65. OPERATIVE REPORT

Preoperative Diagnosis: Basal Cell Carcinoma
Postoperative Diagnosis: Basal Cell Carcinoma
Location: Mid Parietal Scalp

Procedure:

Prior to each surgical stage, the surgical site was tested for anesthesia and re-anesthetized as needed, after which it was prepped and draped in a sterile fashion.

The clinically apparent tumor was carefully defined and de-bulked prior to the first stage, determining the extent of the surgical excision. With each stage, a thin layer of tumor-laden tissue was excised with a narrow margin of normal appearing skin, using the Mohs fresh tissue technique. A map was prepared to correspond to the area of skin from which it was excised. The tissue was prepared for the cryostat and sectioned. Each section was coded, cut and stained for microscopic examination. The surgeon examined the entire base and margins of the excised piece of tissue. Areas noted to be positive on the previous stage (if applicable) were removed with the Mohs technique and processed for analysis.

No tumor was identified after the final stage of microscopically controlled surgery. The patient tolerated the procedure well without any complication. After discussion with the patient regarding the various options, the best closure option for each defect was selected for optimal functional and cosmetic results.

Preoperative Size: 1.5 x 2.9 cm
Postoperative Size: 2.7 x 2.9 cm

Closure: Simple Linear Closure, 3.5cm, scalp

Total # of Mohs Stages: 2

Stage	Sections	Positive
I	6	1
II	2	0

   a. 17311, 17315, 17312, 12002
   b. 17311, 17312, 12002
   c. 17311, 17315, 17312
   d. 17311, 17312

66. A patient with a non-healing burn wound on her right cheek, and is admitted to the OR for surgery. The physician had the patient prepped with a Betadine scrub and draped in the normal sterile fashion. The cheek was anesthetized with 1% Lydocain with 1:800,000 epinephrine (6 cc), and SeptiCare was applied. A skin graft of the epidermis and a small portion of the dermis were taken with a Goulian Weck blade with a six-thousands-of-an-inch-thick shim on the blade. The 25 sq cm graft was flipped and sewn to the adjacent defect with running 5-0 Vicryl. The wound was then dressed with Xeroform and the patient was taken to recovery.
    a. 14041
    b. 15115
    c. 15120
    d. 15758

67. A child is brought into the emergency department after having her fingers on her right hand closed in a car door. The physician evaluates the patient and diagnosis her with a 3cm laceration to her second finger and a subungual hematoma to her third finger. The physician then proceeds to cleanse the fingers with iodine scrub and inject both digits with 2 mL of 1% lidocaine with epinephrine. The wound on the second finger was then irrigated with 500 cc of NS and explored for foreign bodies or structural damage. No foreign bodies were found and tendons and vessels were intact. The wound was then re-approximated. Three 5-0 absorbable mattress sutures were used to close the subcutaneous tissue and six 6-0 nylon interrupted sutures were used to close the epidermis. The finger was then wrapped in sterile gauze and placed in an aluminum finger splint. The physician then check that the digital block performed on the third finger was still effective. After ensuring the patient's finger was still numb he then proceeded to take an electronic cautery unit and created a small hole in the nail. Pressing slightly on the nail he evacuated the hematoma. The hole was then irrigated with 500cc of NS and the finger was wrapped in sterile gauze. The patient tolerated both procedures well without complaint.
    a. 12042-F6, 11740-F7
    b. 64400 (x2), 20103-51, 12042-51, 11740-51,59
    c. 20103, 12042-F6, 11740-F7
    d. 20103, 12042-51, F6, 11740-51, F7

68. The size of an excision of a benign lesion is determined by:
    a. Adding together the lesion diameter and the widest margins necessary to adequately excise the lesion.
    b. Adding together the lesion diameter and the narrowest margins necessary to adequately excise the lesion.
    c. The diameter of the lesion only, excluding any margins excised with it.
    d. The depth of the lesion plus the full diameter of the lesion.

69. A simple, single layered laceration requires extensive cleaning due to being heavily contaminated. The code selected would come from code range 12031-12057.
    a. True
    b. False

70. A skin graft where the donor skin comes from another human (often a cadaver) is known as a/an:
    a. Autograft
    b. Acellulargraft
    c. Allograft
    d. Xenograft

71. A patient is being treated for third degree burns to his left leg and left arm, which cover a total of 18 sq cm. The burns are scrubbed clean, anesthetized, and three incisions are made with a #11 scalpel, through the tough leathery tissue that is dead, in order to expose the fatty tissue below and avoid compartment syndrome. The burns are then re-dressed with sterile gauze.
    a. 97597
    b. 97602
    c. 16035, 16036 x2
    d. 16030, 16035, 16036 x2

Musculoskeletal
20005-29999

72. Medial and lateral meniscus repair performed arthroscopically.
    a. 27447
    b. 29868
    c. 29882
    d. 29883

73. A patient comes into the emergency department complaining of severe wrist pain after falling onto her out stretched hands. The physician evaluates the patient taking a detailed history, a detailed exam, and medical decision making of moderate complexity. Upon examination the physician notes that there is a small portion of bone protruding through the skin. After ordering x-rays of the forearm and wrist the patient is diagnosed with an open distal radius fracture of the right arm. The physician provides an IV drip of morphine to the patient for pain and reduces the fracture. 5-0 absorbable sutures were use to close the subcutaneous layer above the fracture and the surface was closed with 6-0 nylon interrupted sutures. Wound length was measured at 2.5 cm. It was then dressed with sterile gauze and the wrist was stabilized with a Spica fiberglass cast. The physician provided the patient with a prescription for Percocet for pain and instructions for her to follow up with her orthopedist in 7 days.
    a. 99284-25, 25574-RT, 813.52
    b. 99284-57-25, 25605-54-RT, 12031 , 813.52
    c. 99284-57, 25574-54, 813.52
    d. 99284-25, 25605-RT, 12031, 813.52

74. A Scapulopexy is found under what heading
    a. Incision
    b. Excision
    c. Introduction
    d. Repair, Revision, and/or Reconstruction

75. A patient with muscle spasms in her back was seen in her physician's office for treatment. The area over the myofascial spasm was prepped with alcohol utilizing sterile technique. After isolating it between two palpating fingertips a 25-gauge 5" needle was placed in the center of the myofascial spasms and a negative aspiration was performed. Then 4 cc of Marcaine 0.5% was injected into three points in the muscle. The patient tolerated the procedure well without any apparent difficulties or complications. The patient reported feeling full relief by the time the block had set.
    a. 64400
    b. 20552
    c. 64520
    d. 20553

76. OPERATIVE NOTE

PREOPERATIVE DIAGNOSIS: myelopathy secondary to very large disc herniations at C4–C5 and C5–C6.

POSTOPERATIVE DIAGNOSIS: myelopathy secondary to very large disc herniations at C4–C5 and C5–C6.

PROCEDURE PERFORMED:
1. Anterior discectomy, C5–C6.
2. Arthrodesis, C5–C6.
3. Partial corpectomy, C5.
4. Machine bone allograft, C5–C6.
5. Placement of anterior plate with a Zephyr C6.

ANESTHESIA: General.
ESTIMATED BLOOD LOSS: 60 mL.
COMPLICATIONS: None.

INDICATIONS: This is a patient who presents with progressive weakness in the left upper extremity as well as imbalance. He has a very large disc herniation that came behind the body at C5 as well and as well as a large disc herniation at C5–C6. Risks and benefits of the surgery including bleeding, infection, neurologic deficit, nonunion, progressive spondylosis, and lack of improvement were all discussed. He understood and wished to proceed.

DESCRIPTION OF PROCEDURE: The patient was brought to the operating room and placed in the supine position. Preoperative antibiotics were given. The patient was placed in the supine position with all pressure points noted and well padded. The patient was prepped and draped in standard fashion. An incision was made approximately above the level of the cricoid. Blunt dissection was used to expose the anterior portion of the spine with carotid moved laterally and trachea and esophagus moved medially. I then placed needle into the disc spaces and was found to be at C5–C6. Distracting pins were placed in the body of C6. The disc was then completely removed at C5–C6. There was very significant compression of the cord. This was carefully removed to avoid any type of pressure on the cord. This was very severe and multiple free fragments noted. This was taken down to the level of ligamentum. Both foramens were then also opened. Part of the body of C5 was taken down to assure that all fragments were removed and that there was no additional constriction. The nerve root was then widely decompressed. Machine bone allograft was placed into C5–C6 and then a Zephyr plate was placed in the body C6 with a metal pin placed into the body at C5. Excellent purchase was obtained. Fluoroscopy showed good placement and meticulous hemostasis was obtained. Fascia was closed with 3–0 Vicryl, subcuticular 3–0 Dermabond for skin. The patient tolerated the procedure well and went to recovery in good condition.

    a. 22554, 63081, 63082, 20931, 22845
    b. 22551, 63081, 20931, 22840
    c. 22551, 63081, 63082, 20931, 22845
    d. 22554, 63081, 20931, 22840

77. A general surgeon and a neurosurgeon are performing an osteotomy on the L4 vertebral segment. The general surgeon establishes the opening using an anterior approach. While the neurosurgeon performs the osteotomy the general surgeon performs a discectomy. After completion the general surgeon closes the patient up.
    a. General: 22224-59 Neurosurgeon: 22224-54
    b. General: 22224-62 Neurosurgeon: 22224-62
    c. General: 22224-66 Neurosurgeon: 22224-66
    d. General: 22224 Neurosurgeon: 22224-80

78. A patient comes into his physician's office with a prior diagnosis of a Colles type distal radius fracture. He complains that the cast he currently has on is too tight and is causing numbness in his fingers. The physician removes the cast and ensures the patient's circulation is intact. He then re-applies a short arm fiberglass cast and checks the patient's neurovascular status several times during the procedure. The patient is given instructions to follow-up with his orthopedist within seven days.
    a. 25600-77
    b. 25600-52
    c. 29705, 29075
    d. 29075

79. A patient is brought into the OR for a diagnostic arthroscopy of the shoulder. The patient has been complaining of pain since his surgery 4 months ago. The surgeon explores the shoulder and discovers a metal clamp, which had been left in from the prior surgery. The surgeon removed the clamp and closed the patient up.
    a. 29805, 23333
    b. 29805, 29819
    c. 29819-78
    d. 29819

80. This 59 year-old female was brought to the operating room and placed on the surgical table in a supine position. Following anesthesia, the surgical site was prepped and draped in the normal sterile fashion. Attention was then directed to the right foot where, utilizing a # 15 blade, a 6 cm. linear incision was made over the 1st metatarsal head, taking care to identify and retract all vital structures. The incision was medial to and parallel to the extensor hallucis longus tendon. The incision was deepened through subcutaneous underscored, retracted medially and laterally – thus exposing the capsular structures below, which were incised in a linear longitudinal manner, approximately the length of the skin incision. The capsular structures were sharply underscored off the underlying osseous attachments, retracted medially and laterally. Utilizing an osteotome and mallet the medial eminence of the metatarsal bone was removed and the head was remodeled with the Liston bone forceps and the bell rasp. The surgical site was then flushed with saline. The base of the proximal phalanx of the great toe was osteotomized approximately 1 cm distal to the base and excised to toto from the surgical site. There was no hemi implant used and Kirschner wire was used to hold the joint in place. Superficial closure was accomplished using Vicryl 5-0 in a running subcuticular fashion. Site was dressed with a light compressive dressing. The tourniquet was released. Excellent capillary refill to all the digits was observed without excessive bleeding noted.
    a. 28290
    b. 28292
    c. 28294
    d. 28298

81. Operative Note

PREOPERATIVE DIAGNOSIS: Angina and coronary artery disease.
POSTOPERATIVE DIAGNOSIS: Angina and coronary artery disease.

PROCEDURE DETAILS: The patient was brought to the operating room and placed in the supine position upon the table. After adequate general anesthesia, the patient was prepped with Betadine soap and solution in the usual sterile manner. Elbows were protected to avoid ulnar neuropathy and phrenic nerve protectors were used to protect the phrenic nerve. All were removed at the end of the case.

A midline sternal skin incision was made and carried down through the sternum, which was divided with the saw. Pericardial and thymus fat pad was divided. The left internal mammary artery was harvested and spatulated for anastomosis. Heparin was given.

The Femoropopliteal vein was resected from the thigh, side branches secured using 4-0 silk and Hemoclips. The thigh was closed multilayer Vicryl and Dexon technique. A Pulsavac wash was done and a drain was placed.

The left internal mammary artery is sewn to the left anterior descending using 7-0 running Prolene technique with the Medtronic off-pump retractors. After this was done, the patient was fully heparinized, cannulated with a 6.5 atrial cannula and a 2-stage venous catheter and begun on cardiopulmonary bypass and maintained normothermia. Medtronic retractors used to expose the circumflex. Prior to going on pump, we stapled the vein graft in place to the aorta.

Then, on pump, we did the distal anastomosis with a 7-0 running Prolene technique. The right side graft was brought to the posterior descending artery using running 7-0 Prolene technique. Deairing procedure was carried out. The bulldog clamps were removed. The patient maintained good normal sinus rhythm with good mean perfusion. The patient was weaned from cardiopulmonary bypass. The arterial and venous lines were removed and doubly secured. Protamine was delivered. Meticulous hemostasis was present. Platelets were given for coagulopathy. Chest tube was placed and meticulous hemostasis was present. The anatomy and the flow in the grafts was excellent. Closure was begun.

The sternum was closed with wire, followed by linea alba and pectus fascia closure with running 6-0 Vicryl sutures in double-layer technique. The skin was closed with subcuticular 4-0 Dexon suture technique. The patient tolerated the procedure well and was transferred to the intensive care unit in stable condition.

a. 35600, 35572, 33533, 33517, 32551, 36825, 33926
b. 33533, 33517, 35572

c. 33510, 33533, 35572, 32551, 36821
d. 33510, 33533, 33572

82. A 50-year-old gentleman with severe respiratory failure is mechanically ventilated and is currently requiring multiple intravenous drips. With the patient in his Intensive Care Unit bed, mechanically ventilated in the Trendelenburg position, the right neck was prepped and draped with Betadine in a sterile fashion. A single needle stick aspiration of the right subclavian vein was accomplished without difficulty and the guide wire was advanced and a dilator was advanced over the wire. The triple lumen catheter was cannulated over the wire and the wire was then removed. No PVCs were encountered during the procedure. All three ports to the catheter were aspirated and flushed blood easily and they were all flushed with normal saline. The catheter was anchored to the chest wall with butterfly phalange using 3-0 silk suture. Betadine ointment and a sterile Op-Site dressing were applied. Stat upright chest x-ray was obtained at the completion of the procedure to ensure proper placement of the tip in the subclavian vein.
   a. 36557
   b. 36555
   c. 36558
   d. 36556

83. A patient with chronic emphysema has surgery to remove both lobes of the left lung.
   a. 32440
   b. 32482
   c. 32663x2
   d. 32310

84. A thoracic surgeon makes an incision under the sternal notch at the base of the throat, introduces the scope into the mediastinal space and takes two biopsies of the tissue. He then retracts the scope and closes the small incision.
   a. 39400
   b. 32606
   c. 39000
   d. 32405

85. A patient has endoscopic surgery done to remove his anterior and posterior ethmoid sinuses. The surgeon dialated the maxillary sinus with a balloon using a transnasal approach, explored the frontal sinuses, remove two polyps from the maxillary sinus, and then performed the tissue removal.
   a. 31255, 31295, 31237
   b. 31201, 31295, 31237
   c. 31255, 31267
   d. 31255, 31295, 31267

86. **Operative Note**

Approach: Left cephalic vein.

Leads Implanted: Medtronic model 5076-45 in the right atrium, serial number PJN983322V. Medtronic 5076-52 in the right ventricle, serial number PJN961008V.

Device Implanted: Pacemaker, Dual Chamber, Medtronic EnRhythm, model P1501VR, serial number PNP422256H.

Lead Performance: Atrial threshold less than 1.3 volts at 0.5 milliseconds. P wave 3.3 millivolts. Impedance 572 ohms. Right ventricle threshold 0.9 volts at 0.5 milliseconds. R wave 10.3. Impedance 855.

Procedure: The patient was brought to the electrophysiology laboratory in a fasting state and intravenous sedation was provided as needed with Versed and fentanyl. The left neck and chest were prepped and draped in the usual manner and the skin and subcutaneous tissues below the left clavicle were infiltrated with 1% lidocaine for local anesthesia. A 2-1/2-inch incision was made below the left clavicle and electrocautery was used for hemostasis. Dissection was carried out to the level of the pectoralis fascia and extended caudally to create a pocket for the pulse generator. The deltopectoral groove was explored and a medium-sized cephalic vein was identified. The distal end of the vein was ligated and a venotomy was performed. Two guide wires were advanced to the superior vena cava and peel-away introducer sheaths were used to insert the two pacing leads. The venous pressures were elevated and there was a fair amount of back-bleeding from the vein, so a 3-0 Monocryl figure-of-eight stitch was placed around the tissue surrounding the vein for hemostasis. The right ventricular lead was placed in the high RV septum and the right atrial lead was placed in the right atrial appendage. The leads were tested with a pacing systems analyzer and the results are noted above. The leads were then anchored in place with #0-silk around their suture sleeve and connected to the pulse generator. The pacemaker was noted to function appropriately. The pocket was then irrigated with antibiotic solution and the pacemaker system was placed in the pocket. The incision was closed with two layers of 3-0 Monocryl and a subcuticular closure of 4-0 Monocryl. The incision was dressed with Steri-Strips and a sterile bandage and the patient was returned to her room in good condition.

    a. 33240, 33225, 33202
    b. 33208, 33225, 33202
    c. 33213, 33217
    d. 33208

87. If a surgeon is performing a surgical sinus endoscopy to control a nasal hemorrhage and chooses to perform a necessary sinusotomy while he's there, he can bill for each individual service.
    a. True
    b. False

88. A cardiologist manipulates a catheter through the patient's atrial system, starting in the femoral artery and manipulating to the third order, using intravascular ultrasound.
    a. 36217, 37250
    b. 36217, 75945
    c. 36247, 37250
    d. 36247, 75945

89. An indirect laryngoscopy, as described in code 31505, utilizes a mirror in which the physician can view the reflection of the larynx. A direct larngoscopy, as described by code 31515, utilizes a scope in which the physician peers through and views the larynx.
    a. True
    b. False

90. A patient was taken into the operating room where after induction of appropriate anesthesia, her left chest, neck, axilla, and arm were prepped with Betadine solution and draped in a sterile fashion. An incision was made at the hairline and carried down by sharp dissection through the clavipectoral fascia. The lymph node was palpitated in the armpit and grasped with a figure-of-eight 2-0 silk suture and by sharp dissection, was carried to hemoclip all attached structures. The lymph node was excised in its entirety. The wound was irrigated. The lymph node was sent to pathology. The wound was then closed. Hemostasis was assured and the patient was taken to recovery room in stable condition.
    a. 38308
    b. 38500
    c. 38510
    d. 38525

91. The patient was scheduled for an esophagogastroduodenoscopy. Upon arrival they were placed under conscious sedation and instructed to swallow a small flexible camera. The camera was then manipulated into the esophagus, and through the entire length of the esophagus. The esophagus appeared to be slightly inflamed, but there was no sign of erosion or flame hemorrhage. A small 2cm tissue sample was taken to look for gastroesophageal reflux disease. There was no stricture or Barrett mucosa. The bony and the antrum of the stomach were normal without any acute peptic lesions. Retroflexion of the tip of the endoscope in the body of the stomach revealed an abnormal cardia. There were no acute lesions and no evidence of ulcer, tumor, or polyp. The pylorus was easily entered, and the first, second, and third portions of the duodenum were normal.
    a. 43202
    b. 43234
    c. 43235
    d. 43239

92. After informed consent was obtained, the patient was placed in the left lateral decubitus position and sedated. The Olympus video colonoscope was inserted through the anus and was advanced in retrograde fashion through the sigmoid colon, descending colon, and to the splenic flexure. There was a large amount of stool at the flexure, which appeared to be impacted. The physician decided not to advance to the cecum due to the impaction and the scope was pulled back into the descending colon and then slowly withdrawn. The mucosa was examined in detail along the way and was entirely normal. Upon reaching the rectum, retroflex examination of the rectum was normal. The scope was then straightened out, the air removed and the scope withdrawn. The patient tolerated the procedure well.
    a. 45330-53
    b. 45330
    c. 45378-53
    d. 45378

93. **Operative Note**

The 45-year-old male patient was taken to the operative suite, placed on the table in the supine position, and given a spinal anesthetic. The right inguinal region was shaved, prepped, and draped in a routine sterile fashion. The patient received 1 gm of Ancef IV push. A transverse incision was made in the intraabdominal crease and carried through the skin and subcutaneous tissue. The external oblique fascia was exposed and incised down to, and through, the external inguinal ring. The spermatic cord and hernia sac were dissected bluntly off the undersurface of the external oblique fascia exposing the attenuated floor of the inguinal canal. The cord was surrounded with a Penrose drain. The sac was separated from the cord structures. The floor of the inguinal canal, which consisted of attenuated transversalis fascia, was imbricated upon itself with a running locked suture of 2-0 Prolene. Marlex patch 1 x 4 in dimension was trimmed to an appropriate shape with a defect to accommodate the cord. It was placed around the cord and sutured to itself with 2-0 Prolene. The patch was then sutured medially to the pubic tubercle, inferiorly to Cooper's ligament and inguinal ligaments, and superiorly to conjoined tendon using 2-0 Prolene. The area was irrigated with saline solution, and 0.5% Marcaine with epinephrine was injected to provide prolonged postoperative pain relief. The cord was returned to its position. External oblique fascia was closed with a running 2-0 PDS, subcu with 2-0 Vicryl, and skin with running subdermal 4-0 Vicryl and Steri-Strips. Sponge and needle counts were correct. Sterile dressing was applied.
   a. 49505
   b. 49505, 54520
   c. 49505, 49568
   d. 49505,54520, 49568

94. The vestibule is part of the oral cavity outside the dentoalveolar structures and includes the mucosal and submucosal tissue of the lips and cheeks.
   a. True
   b. False

95. Which of the following organs is not part of the alimentary canal?
   a. Gallbladder
   b. Duodenum
   c. Jejunum
   d. Tounge

96. A 13-year-old child has his tonsils and adenoids removed due acute tonsillitis and chronic tonsilitis and adenoiditis.
   a. 42826, 42831, 475, 474.0
   b. 42826, 42836, 463, 474.02
   c. 42821, 463, 474.02
   d. 42821-50, 463, 474.0

97. **Operative Note**

Preoperative Diagnosis: Protein-calorie malnutrition
Postoperative Diagnosis: Protein-calorie malnutrition.
Anesthesia: Conscious sedation per Anesthesia..
Complications: None
EGD: Dr. Brown
PEG Placement: Dr. Smith

History: The patient is a 73-year-old male who was admitted to the hospital with some mentation changes. He was unable to sustain enough caloric intake and had markedly decreased albumin stores. After discussion with the patient and his son they agreed to place a PEG tube for nutritional supplementation.

Procedure: After informed consent was obtained the patient was brought to the endoscopy suite. He was placed in the supine position and was given IV sedation by the Anesthesia Department. Dr. Brown, who has dictated his finding separately, performed an EGD from above. The stomach was transilluminated and an optimal position for the PEG tube was identified using the single poke method. The skin was infiltrated with local and the needle and sheath were inserted through the abdomen into the stomach under direct visualization. The needle was removed and a guidewire was inserted through the sheath. Dr.Brown grasped the guidewire with a snare from above. It was removed completely and the Ponsky PEG tube was secured to the guidewire. The guidewire and PEG tube were then pulled through the mouth and esophagus and snug to the abdominal wall. There was no evidence of bleeding. Photos were taken. The Bolster was placed on the PEG site. Dr. Brown will do a complete dictation for the EGD separately. The patient tolerated the procedure well and was transferred to recovery room in stable condition. He will be started on tube feedings in 6 hours with aspiration and dietary precautions to determine his nutritional goal.

What code(s) should Dr. Smith charge?
   a. 43246-62
   b. 49440
   c. 43752
   d. 43653

98. An 18-year-old female was found with a suicide note and an empty bottle of Tylenol. She was rushed into the emergency department where she had a large-bore gastric lavage tube inserted into her stomach and the contents were evacuated.
   a. 43756
   b. 43752
   c. 43753
   d. 43754

99. All endoscopies performed on the digestive system (such as an esophagoscopy, a colonoscopy, a sigmoidoscopy, etc.) do not allow moderate sedation to be coded additionally because it is bundled into the code?
    a. True
    b. False

100.   **Operative Note**
    History of Present Illness: Ms. Moore is status post lap band placement, the band was placed just over a year ago and she is here for a lap band adjustment. She has a history of problems previously with her adjustments. She has been under a lot of stress recently due to a car accident she was in a couple of weeks ago. Since the accident she has been experiencing problems of "not feeling full". She states that she is not really hungry but she does not feel full either. She also states that when she is hungry at night she is having difficulty waiting until the morning to eat. She also mentioned that she had a candy bar and that seemed to make her feel better.

    Physical Examination: On exam, her temperature is 98, pulse 76, weight 197.7 pounds, blood pressure 102/72, BMI is 38.5, she has lost 3.8 pounds since her last visit. She was alert and oriented in no apparent distress.

    Procedure: I was able to access her port. She does have an AP standard low profile. I aspirated 6 mL, I did add 1 mL, so she has got approximately 7 mL in her restrictive device, and she did tolerate water post procedure.

    Assessment: The patient's status post lap band adjustments; doing well, has a total of 7 mL within her lap band, tolerated water pos procedure. She will come back in two weeks for another adjustment as needed.
    a. 43771
    b. 43886
    c. 43842
    d. 43848

101. A patient was brought to the OR and sedated. She was then placed in the supine position on a water filled cushion. The C-Arm image intensifier was positioned in the correct anatomical location above the left renal and a total of 2500 high energy shock waves were applied from the outside of the body. Energy levels were slowly started and O2 increased up to 7. Gradually the 2.5cm stone was broken into smaller pieces as the number of shocks went up. The shocks were started at 60 per minute and slowly increased up to 90 per minute. The patient's heart rate and blood pressure were stable throughout the entire procedure. She was transported to recovery in good condition.
   a. 50081, 74425
   b. 50130, 76770
   c. 50060
   d. 50590

102. A patient recently underwent a total hysterectomy due to ovarian cancer, which has metastasized. She is now having cylinder rods placed for clinical brachytherapy treatment. Treatment will consist of high dose rate (HDR) brachytherapy once correct placement of the rods has been confirmed.
   a. 57155
   b. 57156
   c. 57155-58
   d. 57156-58

103. The patient was brought to the suite, where after oral sedation; the scrotum was prepped and draped. 1% lidocaine was used for local anesthesia. The vas was identified, skin was incised, and no scalpel instruments were used to dissect out the vas. A segment about 3 cm in length was dissected out. It was clipped proximally and distally, and then the ends were cauterized after excising the segment. Minimal bleeding was encountered and the scrotal skin was closed with 3-0 chromic. The identical procedure was performed on the contralateral side. The patient tolerated the procedure well. He was discharged from the surgical center in good condition with Tylenol with Codeine for pain.
   a. 55450
   b. 55400
   c. 55400-50
   d. 55250

104.   **Operative Note**

Epidural anesthesia was administered in the holding area, after which the patient was transferred into the operating room. General endotracheal anesthesia was administered, after which the patient was positioned in the flank standard position. A left flank incision was made over the area of the twelfth rib. The subcutaneous space was opened by using the Bovie. The ribs were palpated clearly and the fascia overlying the intercostal space between the eleventh and twelfth rib was opened by using the Bovie. The fascial layer covering of the intercostal space was opened completely until the retroperitoneum was entered. Once the retroperitoneum had been entered, the incision was extended until the peritoneal envelope could be identified. The peritoneum was swept medially. The Finochietto retractor was then placed for exposure. The kidney was readily identified and was mobilized from outside Gerota's fascia. The ureter was dissected out easily and was separated with a vessel loop. The superior aspect of the kidney was mobilized from the superior attachment. The pedicle of the left kidney was completely dissected revealing the vein and the artery. The artery was a single artery and was dissected easily by using a right-angle clamp. A vessel loop was placed around the renal artery. The tumor could be easily palpated in the lateral lower pole to mid pole of the left kidney. The Gerota's fascia overlying that portion of the kidney was opened in the area circumferential to the tumor. Once the renal capsule had been identified, the capsule was scored using a Bovie about 0.5 cm lateral to the border of the tumor. Bulldog clamp was then placed on the renal artery. The tumor was then bluntly dissected off of the kidney with a thin rim of a normal renal cortex. This was performed by using the blunted end of the scalpel. The tumor was removed easily. The argon beam coagulation device was then utilized to coagulate the base of the resection. The visible larger bleeding vessels were oversewn by using 4-0 Vicryl suture. The edges of the kidney were then reapproximated by using 2-0 Vicryl suture with pledgets at the ends of the sutures to prevent the sutures from pulling through. Two horizontal mattress sutures were placed and were tied down. The Gerota's fascia was then also closed by using 2-0 Vicryl suture. The area of the kidney at the base was covered with Surgicel prior to tying the sutures. The bulldog clamp was removed and perfect hemostasis was evident. There was no evidence of violation into the calyceal system. A 19-French Blake drain was placed in the inferior aspect of the kidney exiting the left flank inferior to the incision. The drain was anchored by using silk sutures. The flank fascial layers were closed in three separate layers in the more medial aspect. The lateral posterior aspect was closed in two separate layers using Vicryl sutures. The skin was finally re-approximated by using metallic clips. The patient tolerated the procedure well.
   a. 50545
   b. 50240
   c. 50220
   d. 50290

105.   A 26-year-old patient who is Gravida 2 Para 1 presents to the ER in her 36th week of pregnancy with twin gestations that are monochorionic and monoamniotic. She is in active labor, 6 cm dilated, and her water is intact. Her OBGYN, who provided 12 antepartum visits, admitted her to labor & delivery. Although the patient had a previous cesarean during her first pregnancy the physician allowed her to attempt a vaginal birth. After pushing for three hours the patient was exhausted and taken to the OR for a cesarean delivery with a transverse incision. Two healthy newborns were born 15 minutes later. During the hospital stay and afterward the same physician provided the postpartum care to the mother.
   a. 59426, 59622,59620, 651.01, 644.21, V31.1, V91.01
   b. 59618, 59620-51, 651.01, 644.21,669.71, V27.2, V91.01
   c. 59618, 59618-51, 651.01, V27.2, V91.01
   d. 59618-22, 669.71, 644.21, V31.1, V91.01

106.   When reporting delivery only services the discharge should be reported by using an E/M.
   a. True
   b. False

107.   A 74-year-old male with a weak urinary stream had his PSA tested. Results read 12.5 and he was scheduled for a biopsy to determine whether he had a malignancy or BPH. He arrived for surgery and was placed in the left lateral decubitus position and he was sedated. The surgeon used ultrasonic guidance to percutaneously retrieve 3 biopsies, using the transperineal approach. The biopsies were examined and the patient was diagnoised with secondary prostate cancer with the primary site unknown. He was directed to schedule a PET scan and discharged in good condition.
   a. 55875, 76965
   b. 55706, 76942
   c. 55700, 76942
   d. 55705, 76942

108.   **Procedure:** Hydrocelectomy

A scrotal incision was made and further extended with electrocautery. Once the hydrocele sac was reached we then opened and delivered the testis which drained clear fluid. There was moderate amount of scarring on the testis itself from the tunica vaginalis. The hydrocele sac was completely removed. A drain was then placed in the base of the scrotum and then the testis was placed back into the scrotum in the proper orientation. The same procedure was performed on the left. The skin was then sutured with a running interlocking suture of 3-0 Vicryl and the drains were sutured to place with 3-0 Vicryl. Bacitracin dressing, ABD dressing, and jock strap were placed. The patient was in stable condition upon transfer to recovery.
   a. 55041
   b. 54861
   c. 55000-50
   d. 55060

109.   A urologist performs a cystometrogram with intra-abdominal voiding pressure studies in a hospital using calibrated electronic equipment that is provided for his use. He interprets the study and diagnosis the patient with neurogenic bladder.
   a. 51726, 51797
   b. 51729-26, 51797-26
   c. 51726-26, 51797-26
   d. 51729, 51797

110.   Transvaginal sonographically controlled **retrieval of a 26-year-old female's eggs by** piercing the ovarian follicle with a very fine needle.
   a. 58976, 76948
   b. 58672
   c. 58970, 76948
   d. 58940, 76948

111.   The hammer, anvil, and stirrup are the English terms for the three auditory ossicles, whose Latin names are:
   a. Stapes, Utricle, and cochlea
   b. Malleus, incus, and stapes
   c. Utricle, incus, and vestibular nerve
   d. Malleus, stapes, Utricle

112.   **Operative Note**

Pre-operative Diagnosis: Increased intracranial pressure and cerebral edema due to severe brain injury.

Post operative Diagnosis: Increased intracranial pressure and cerebral edema due to severe brain injury.

Procedure: Scalp was clipped. Patient was prepped with ChloraPrep and Betadine. Incisions are infiltrated with 1% Xylocaine with epinephrine 1:200000. Patient did receive antibiotics post procedure and was draped in a sterile manner.The incision made just to the right of the right mid-pupillary line 10 cm behind the nasion. A self-retaining retractor was placed. A hole was then drilled with the cranial twist drill and the dura was punctured. A brain needle was used to localize the ventricle and it took 3 passes to localize the ventricle. The pressure was initially high. The CSF was clear and colorless. The CSF drainage rapidly tapered off because of the brain swelling. With two tries, the ventricular catheter was then able to be placed into the ventricle and then brought out through a separate puncture site; the depth of catheter was 7 cm from the outer table of the skull. There was intermittent drainage of CSF after that. The catheter was secured to the scalp with #2-0 silk sutures and the incision was closed with Ethilon suture. The patient tolerated the procedure well. No complications. Sponge and needle counts were correct. Blood loss is minimal.
   a. 61107, 62160
   b. 61210
   c. 61107
   d. 61210, 62160

113.   Using the posterior approach the surgeon made a midline incision above the underlying vertebrae and dissected down to the paravertabral muscles and retracted then. The ligamentum flavum, lamina, and fragments of a ruptured C3-C4 intervertebral disc were all removed. The surgeon also removed a portion of the facet to relieve the compressed nerve of the C4 vertebrae. He then placed a free-fat graft over the exposed nerve and the paravertabral muscles were repositioned. The patient was then closed using layered sutures and taken to recovery.
   a. 63040
   b. 63075
   c. 63081
   d. 63170

114.   A procedure in which corneal tissue from a donor is frozen, reshaped, and implanted into the anterior corneal stroma of the recipient to modify refractive error.
   a. 65710
   b. 65760
   c. 65765
   d. 65770

115.   Which of the following organs is not part of the endocrine system
   a. Thyroid
   b. Pancreas
   c. Lymph nodes
   d. Adrenal Glands

116.   Using an operating microscope the ophthalmologist places stay sutures into the rectus muscle. A cold probe is then placed over the sclera and is depressed sealing the choroid to the retina at the original tear site. He then performs a sclerotomy and places mattress sutures across the incision. Subretinal fluid is then drained. Next a silicone sponge, followed by a silicone band, are placed around the eye and sutured into place to help support the healing scar. Rectus sutures are removed.
   a. 67101
   b. 671101, 69990
   c. 67107
   d. 67107, 69990

117. Following a motor vehicle collision a 28-year-old male was given a CT scan of the brain which indicated an infratentorial hematoma in the cerebellum. The patient was taken to the OR where the neurosurgeon, using the CT coordinates, incised the scalp and drilled a burr hole into the cranium above the hematoma. Under direct visualization he then evacuated the hematoma using suction and irrigated with NS. Hemorrhaging was controlled and the dura was closed. The skull piece was then placed back into the drill hole and screwed into place. The scalp was closed and the patient was sent to recovery.
   a. 61154
   b. 61253, 61315
   c. 61315
   d. 61154, 61315

118. An incision was made right in the mid palm area between the thenar and hypothenar eminence. Meticulous hemostasis of any bleeders was done. The fat was identified. The palmar aponeurosis was identified and cut and this was traced down to the wrist. There was severe compression of the median nerve. Additional removal of the aponeurosis was performed to allow for further decompression. After this was all completed, the area was irrigated with saline and bacitracin solution and closed as a single layer using Prolene 4-0 as interrupted vertical mattress stitches. Dressing was applied. The patient was brought to the recovery.
   a. 64702
   b. 64704
   c. 64719
   d. 64721

119. A postaurical incision is made on the right ear. With the use of an operating microscope the surgeon visualizes and reflects the skin flap and posterior eardrum forward. A small leak from the middle ear into the round window is noted. The surgeon then roughens up the surface of the window and packs it with fat. Upon retraction the eardrum and skin flap are replaced and the canal is packed. The surgeon then sutures the postaurical incision. He then repeats the procedure on the left ear.
   a. 69666-50, 69990
   b. 69667-50, 69990
   c. 69666, 69990
   d. 69667-50

120. Code 60512 should not be used:
   a. In conjunction with code 60260
   b. As a primary code
   c. As an additional code following a total thyroidectomy
   d. After code 60500

121.   Some radiology codes include two components. Often a radiologist will
        use the radiology equipment, which is known as the technical component, and
        the physician will provide the second half of the CPT code by supervising and
        interpreting the study. When this occurs what should the physician report?
        a. The full CPT code
        b. The CPT code with a modifier TC
        c. The CPT with a modifier 26
        d. The CPT with a modifier 52

122.   A patient presents to the ER with intractable nausea and vomiting, and
        abdominal pain that radiates into her pelvis. The physician orders a CT scan of
        the abdomen, first without contrast and then followed by contrast, and a CT of
        the pelvis, without contrast.
        a. 74178
        b. 74178, 74176-51
        c. 74178 x2, 74177
        d. 74176, 74178-51

123.   A patient was in an MVA and his face struck the steering wheel. He had
        multiple contusions and facial swelling. The physician suspected a zygomatic-
        malar or maxilla fracture. The radiologist took an oblique anterior-posterior
        projection, which showed the facial complex clearly. Anterior-posterior and
        lateral views were also taken.
        a. 70100
        b. 70120
        c. 70150
        d. 70250

124.   If a prior study is available but it is documented in the medical records
        that there was inadequate visualization of the anatomy, then a diagnostic
        angiography may be reported in conjunction with an interventional procedure if
        modifier 59 is appended to the diagnostic S&I.
        a. True
        b. False

125.   A physician performed a deep bone biopsy of the femur. The trocar was
        visualized and guided using a CAT scan and interpretation was provided.
        a. 20245, 77012-26
        b. 20225, 77012
        c. 38221, 76998
        d. 20225, 73700

126.   HDR internal radiation therapy was performed by using a remote
        controlled MultiSource afterloader, which was connected to 3 catheters. The 6
        Ir-192 radioactive wire sources were released from the containment unit and
        were delivered beside the tumor within the body cavity, as pre-determined.
        After 15 minutes the sources were removed from the patient and placed back
        into the containment unit.
        a. 77762
        b. 77790
        c. 77786
        d. 77777

127.   A patient has a myocardial perfusion imaging study which included
        quantitative wall motion, ejection fraction by gated technique, and attenuation
        correction. The study was done during a cardiac stress test which was induced
        by using dipyridamole. The physician supervised, the interpretation and report
        were completed by the cardiologist.
        a. 78451, 93016
        b. 78453, 93016
        c. 78451
        d. 78453

128.   A 35-year-old mother carrying twin gestations, who has a three-year-old
        child with Down syndrome, comes in for a prenatal screening. She is in her 12th
        week of pregnancy and the physician requests that the amount of fluid behind
        the necks of the fetuses be measured. A transabdominal approach was used.
        a. 76801, 76802
        b. 76811, 76812
        c. 76813, 76814
        d. 76816, 76816-59

129.   A dialysis patient presents in the radiology department. His physician
        suspects that the tip of his Hickman's catheter in his left forearm may have
        migrated from its original placement. The vascular surgeon on-call injects
        radiopaque iodine into the patient's port and examines it under fluoroscopic
        imaging.
        a. 36598
        b. 36598, 75820
        c. 36598, 75820, 76000
        d. 75820

130.   A written report signed by the interpreting physician should be
        considered an integral part of the radiological procedure or interpretation.
        a. True
        b. False

131.   A physician orders a patient's blood be tested for levels of urea nitrogen, sodium, potassium, transferase alanine and aspartate amnio, total protein, ionized calcium, carbon dioxide, chloride, creatinine, glucose, and TSH.
a. 80053-52, 84443
b. 80048, 84443, 84155, 84460, 84450
c. 80047, 84460, 84450, 84155, 84443
d. 80051, 84520, 84460, 84450, 84155, 82330, 82565, 82947, 84443

132.   A specimen labeled "right ovarian cyst" is received for examination. It consists of a smooth-walled, clear fluid filled cyst measuring 13x12x7 cm and weighing 1351 grams with fluid. Both surfaces of the wall are pink-tan, smooth and grossly unremarkable. No firm or thick areas or papillary structures are noted on the cyst wall externally or internally. After removal the fluid, the cyst weight 68 grams. The fluid is transparent and slightly mucoid.
a. 88300
b. 88304
c. 88305
d. 88307

133.   A patient presents to the ED with chest pain, shortness of breath, and a history of congestive heart failure. The physician performs a 12 lead EKG which indicates a myocardial infarction without ST elevations. The physician immediately orders myoglobin, quantitative troponin, and CK enzyme levels to be run once every hour for three consecutive hours.
a. 83874-99, 83874-76, 83874-91, 84484-99, 84484-76, 84484-91, 82250-99, 82250-76, 82250-91
b. 83874, 83874-91 x2, 84484, 84484-91 x2, 82550, 82550-91 x2
c. 83874-91 x3, 84484-91 x3, 82250-91 x3
d. 83874 x3, 84484 x3, 82550 x3

134.   A 17-year-old female presents in her family physician's office complaining of nausea, vomiting, and weight gain. She has been experiencing these symptoms on and off for two weeks. An analysis of the urine reveals a positive pregnancy test and hCG levels of 12500 mIU/ml confirm she is in her sixth week of pregnancy.
a. 81005, 84702
b. 81025, 84702
c. 81025, 84703
d. 81005, 84703

135.   An employee was randomly selected for a drug screen. According to the employer it is standard procedure to use a multiplex screening kit and test for barbiturates, cocaine, opiates, and methadone. Any drug with a positive result should be confirmed with a second, quantitative test. The employee showed positive for barbiturates and opiates. Secondary tests were run on the two and levels came back with 350 ng/ml for barbituates and 375 ng/ml for opiates.
   a. 80101, 80101-91 x3, 80102, 80102-91
   b. 80104, 80104-91 x3, 80102, 80102-91
   c. 80100, 80100-91 x3, 82205, 83925
   d. 80104,82205, 83925

136.   A CBC does not include which of the following:
   a. RBC
   b. Hgb
   c. hCG
   d. WBC

137.   A couple that was unsuccessful at conceiving a child chooses to have in vitro fertilization done. The eggs and semen have been harvested and nine eggs were implanted with a sperm. The zygotes went through mitosis and produced embryos. Three embryos were then implanted in the woman and the other six were kept for later use. What codes(s) would the lab technician charge for her services in preserving the remaining six embryos?
   a. 89255 x6
   b. 89258
   c. 89268
   d. 89342

138.   A patient in her 30th week of pregnancy has a high oral glucose reading and her physician orders a glucose tolerance test. Upon arrival the laboratory technician draws the patient's blood and the patient then ingests a glucose drink. Her blood is then drawn one, two, and three hours after the ingestion. As the patient was leaving the laboratory the technician informs her that the samples were incorrectly labeled and that the test needed to be repeated. The patient has her blood drawn again, ingested the glucose drink again, and has her blood re-drawn at one, two, and three hour intervals.
   a. 82951, 82951-91
   b. 82946, 82946-91
   c. 82947, 82950, 82950-91 x2
   d. 82951

139.   Carbon dioxide, total calcium, and sodium and all in what three panels?
   a. 82374, 82310, 84295
   b. 80069, 80047, 80048
   c. 80048, 80053, 80069
   d. 80047, 80069, 80051

140.   A qualitative hCG test will provide a positive or negative result while a quantitative hCH test will provide a specific amount of hCG in the specimen.
   a. True
   b. False

141.   A 5-year-old is brought into the ER after being attacked by a stray dog. The stray was captured and tested positive for rabies. The patient has a 3cm laceration on his right cheek that requires simple closure and a 1cm and 4cm laceration on his upper left arm requiring layered repair. After discussing the benefits and risks with the patient's parents they decide to have an IM rabies vaccination administered by the physician, due to the patient's rabies exposure.
    a. 873.41, 880.03, V04.5, 12013, 12031-51, 12032-51, 96372-51, 90375
    b. 873.41, 880.09, V01.5, 12032, 12013-51, 90460-51, 90675
    c. 873.41, 880.09, V04.5, 12032, 12013-51, 90471-51, 90675-51
    d. 873.41, 880.09, V01.5, 12032, 12013-51, 90460-51, 90375

142.   A 52-year-old male is in the emergency department complaining of dizziness and states he passed out prior to arrival. The physician evaluates him, orders that a 12 lead EKG be performed, and has the nurse infuse 2 liters of NS over a 1 hour and 45 minute time period under his supervision. The EKG results were reviewed by the physician and were normal. A report was written and the patient was diagnosed with syncope due to dehydration and released. In addition to the EM service what should the physician code for?
    a. 93010, 96360, 96361
    b. 93000, 96360
    c. 93010
    d. 93000, 96360, 96361

143.   A 45-year-old patient with end stage renal disease has in home dialysis services initiated on the 15th of the month. The physician provides dialysis every day. On the 19th the patient was admitted to the hospital and discharged on the 24th. The physician and patient began in-home dialysis again on the 25th and continued every day until the 31st.
    a. 90960
    b. 90966
    c. 90970
    d. 90970 x11

144.   A patient with a dual lead implantable cardioverter-defibrillator has his physician initiate remote monitoring of the ICD and of cardiovascular monitor functionality (within the ICD), to help diagnosis the patient with what he suspects is left sided heart failure. Over the course of 90 days the physician remotely analyzes recorded data from the device, including left atrial pressure, ventricular pressure, and the patient's blood pressure. He also remotely analyzes data from the defibrillator, including the heart rhythms and pace. After analysis and review the physician compiles reports on both. During this time period there was also one in-person interrogation of the ICM device and one in-person encounter for programming and adjusting the ICD device to ensure test functions and to optimize programming.

    a. 93297 x3, 93295, 93290, 93283
    b. 93297, 93295, 93290, 93283
    c. 93297, 93295, 93283
    d. 93297 x3, 93295, 93283

145.   **History:** Past ocular surgery history is significant for neurovascular age-related dry macular degeneration. Patient has had laser four times to the macula on the right and two times to the left.

Exam: Established 63-year-old female patient. On examination, lids, surrounding tissues, and palpebral fissure are all unremarkable. Conjunctiva, sclera, cornea and iris were all assessed as well. Palpitation of the orbital rim revealed nothing. Visual acuity with correction measured 20/400 OU. Manifest refraction did not improve this. There was no afferent pupillary defect. Visual fields were grossly full to hand motions. Intraocular pressure measured 17 mm in each eye. Vertical prism bars were used to measure ocular deviation and a full sensorimotor examination to evaluate the function of the ocular motor system was performed. A slit-lamp examination was significant for clear corneas OU. There was early nuclear sclerosis in both eyes. There was a sheet like 1-2+ posterior subcapsular cataract on the left. Dilated examination by way of cycloplegia showed choroidal neovascularization with subretinal heme and blood in both eyes. Magnified inspection was obtained with a Goldman 3-mirror lens and the retina, optic disc, and retinal vasculature were visualized. Macular degeneration was present in both the left and right retinas.

Assessment/Plan: Advanced neurovascular age-related macular degeneration OU, this is ultimately visually limiting. Cataracts are present in both eyes. I doubt cataract removal will help increase visual acuity; however, I did discuss with the patient, especially in the left, that cataract surgery will help us better visualize the macula for future laser treatment so that her current vision can be maintained. We discussed her current regiments and decided to continue with the high doses of the vitamins A, C and E, and the minerals zinc and copper to help slow her degeneration. After consideration the patient agreed to left cataract surgery, which we scheduled for two weeks from today.
    a. 92012
    b. 92014
    c. 92014, 92060
    d. 92012, 92060, 92081

146.   Some procedures or services are commonly carried out as an integral component of another total service or procedure and are identified by the inclusion term "separate procedure". Codes with this inclusion term should not be reported in addition to the total procedure code or service to which it is considered an integral part, unless it is independently carried out or considered unrelated. If performed independently or as an un-related procedure it may be coded with modifier 59 appended to it.
    a. True
    b. False

147. A 73-year-old group home resident with end stage renal disease has a nurse come in on Mondays, Wednesdays, and Fridays to perform peritoneal dialysis. Each dialysis session lasts three hours. Once a week, (on Friday), the nurse also assists the patient with his meals, cleaning, and grocery shopping. What should the nurse charge for a month (30 days) of services if the 1st of the month landed on a Monday?
   a. 99601, 99602 x25, 99509 x4
   b. 99601 x13, 99602 x13, 99509 x4
   c. 90966, 99509 x4
   d. 99512 x 13, 99509 x4

148. The physician performs a non-imaging physiological recording of pressure on the left leg with Doppler analysis of blood flow in both directions. ABIs were taken at the back and front lower aspect of the tibial and tibial/dorsalis pedis arteries. In addition 2 levels of plethymography volume and oxygen tension were taken.
   a. 93923-52
   b. 93923
   c. 93922
   d. 93922-52

149. Due to a suspected gastric outlet obstruction a manometric study is performed. Using nuclear medicine the physician monitors the time it takes for food to move through the patient's stomach, the time it take the patient's stomach to empty into the small intestine, and how fully it empties.
   a. 91010
   b. 91020
   c. 91022
   d. 0242T

150. Which of the following drugs is not pending FDA approval?
   a. 90664
   b. 90665
   c. 90666
   d. 90667

Medical Coding Answer Key With Rationale

Medical terminology

1. **B** - Cutting into is the term "otomy"; Surgical removal is the "ectomy"; A permanent opening is the term "ostomy"; Surgical repair is the term "plasty". Some CPT books have common medical terms like these listed in the first few pages of the book.

2. **C** - In your CPT book turn to the index and look up the word vaccination. Indented beneath vaccination look for the abbreviation MMRV or the word Measles. You will see the full description "Measles, Mumps, Rubella, and Varicella" and beneath it you will see the abbreviation MMRV.

3. **D** - Each term listed can be looked up in the CPT book's index (if they do not exist in the index move to the next one). Beside the term magnetic resonance imaging you will see the abbreviation MRI.

4. **A** - Knowing some medical terminology is useful here. The term "salp" means tube, the term "ooph" refers to the ovary, and the suffix "ectomy" means to surgically remove. Some CPT books have common medical terms like these listed in the first few pages of the book.

5. **D** - This is a rare occasion when the answer is not located in one of the medical coding books. I do know that this question (or one similar to it) often appears on the exam. I suggest writing out the meaning of this acronym in coding guidelines for the eyes/ears just before the code sets (65091-69990), or in the notes section just after the code sets.

6. **C** - The prefix "cryo" means cold, as in freezing.

7. **D** - The medical suffix -centesis means to puncture. Arthrocentesis is the puncturing and removal of fluid from a joint. Amniocentesis is the puncturing and removal of amniotic fluid from the amniotic sac during pregnancy. Pericardiocentesis is the puncturing of the pericardium (sac surrounding the heart) and removing extra fluid with it. Paracentisis is the puncturing and removal of fluid from within a body cavity.

8. **B** - The medical prefix gastro means stomach. The medical suffix -ectomy (option A) means to remove. The suffix -otomy (option B) means to cut into. The suffix -ostomy (option C) means to create a permanent

opening. The suffix -rrhaphy (option D) means to suture. Some CPT books have common medical terms like these listed in the first few pages of the book.

9. A - The term nephro and the term renal both refer to the kidney. Examples: nephrolithasis (a kidney stone); renal calculi (a kidney stone).

10.   B- The medical prefix myo- means muscle.

Anatomy

11.   C - There are a few ways to look up anatomy questions. If your CPT book is issued by the AMA (the most common CPT book) and is either the professional or expert edition, then there is an anatomical chart for each organ system located with the coding guidelines for each number set. In this case a skeleton diagram would be located in the coding guidelines just before the musculoskeletal codes (20005-29999). If you do not have this diagram try looking up the word radius either in the CPT or ICD-9 index and find a code or a few codes near that term. Flip to those codes and look for a diagram.

12.   B - The answer to this question can be found the same two ways as the explanation above describes

13.   C - Some CPT books will have a few diagrams located in the front of the CPT book. These diagrams describe body planes, regions, quadrant, and directional terms (Ex. Posterior). If your book does not contain these diagrams try looking up the term "femur, fracture, and then each term (distal, etc.)" in the index. The terms that do not exist in the index should indicate they are not the correct answer. Flip to the code provided for the terms that are in the index and look at any anatomical diagrams. Ex. Femur, fracture, distal gives codes 27508, 27510, and 27514. If a diagram is not provided remember that CPT codes are sequenced from the top of the body down, so code 27508 is closer to the hip (top of the body) and code 27514 is closer to the knee.

14.   D - Again, look for an anatomical diagram first. Either in the front of the CPT or in the guidelines of the digestive system. If no diagrams are provided in your book then try looking up the term "abdominal" in your CPT or ICD-9 book and search for diagrams or wording to help you.

15.   B - This is another occasion that either you will find the answer in the diagrams in the front of your CPT book, or your book does not provide them. If you do not have these diagrams then this question would need to be an educated guess. Knowing medical terminology could also assist here. In this case the term *mid* means middle.

16.   D - Prior to the digestive system coding guidelines is a diagram of the digestive system that labels the duodenum (where the stomach first empties into the small intestine), the Ileum, and the Jejunum. The cecum is also labeled; however, this is part of the large intestine.

17.   C - The round window is located in the inner ear and the oval window is located in the middle ear. A surgeon can also create a pericardial window in the sac surrounding the heart. If the term "round window" were looked up in the CPT index you would be lead to code 69666 in the auditory system. Diagrams for code 69930 would indicate the location of the round window.

18.   B - Distal is the point of an organ or body part farthest from the point of attachment. The term lateral means "away from the midline of the body" and the term Medial means "toward the midline of the body.

19.   C - The temporalis is located in the jaw and helps to move the tempromandubular joint. The trapezius muscle extends from the occipital bone down along the thoracic vertebrae. The teres the deltoid and the four muscles that make up the rotator cuff are the six major muscles of the scapularhumeral group. The trigone muscle is a triangular smooth muscle sensitive to expansion and in charge of signaling to the brain when relief is needed.

20.   B - The cardia fundus is the junction that joins the cardia (the top portion of the stomach closest to the heart) with the esophagus. The Latin term fundus means the portion of an organ opposite from its opening (referring to the opposite end of the esophagus opening and/or the portion of the stomach named the fundus, which is beside the stomach opening and across from the stomach outlet).

Coding Concepts

21. **A** - Just prior to code 22840 there are some code specific coding guidelines. In the third paragraph it states, "do not append modifier 62 to spinal instrumentation codes 22840-22848 and 22850-20938".

22. **B** - ABN stands for advanced beneficiary notice, and is a document that a patient signs stating that they will pay for the procedure they are having done if insurance does not cover it. This is something taught in a medical billing and/or coding class, or something read in preparation of the exam. This answer is not located in one of the coding books.

23. **D** - Wound exploration codes are 20100-20103. Directly above these codes is the wound exploration coding guidelines. In the guidelines it states that the following components are part of the codes description: surgical exploration and enlargement of the wound, extension of dissection, debridement, removal of foreign bodies, ligation or coagulation of minor subcutaneous and/or muscular blood vessel(s).

24. **C** - In the CPT book there are two types of descriptions: common and unique. The common portion of a descriptor follows a code and end with a semi-colon (;). Any CPT that share that description is indented beneath the code. Any portion of the description following the semi-colon is the "Unique" portion of the descriptor and only belongs to a single code. In this case code 24900 contains the common descriptor "Amputation, arm through humerus". Codes 24920 through 24931 share that part of the description and so are indented beneath it with their unique portion of the descriptor beside them.

25. **C** - Medical necessity is what adjudicates, or justifies, a claim for payment. If a physician wants to be paid for a laceration repair (CPT), then the ICD-9 code needs to describe a situation that says it is necessary (ICD-9 should be a laceration or open wound).

26. **D** - Late effects codes are a type of E code. E codes and add on codes are never primary codes and should never be coded by themselves. While V codes are not normally coded as primary or stand alone codes they can be in certain circumstance.

27.   D - Appendix E lists all CPT codes that are modifier 51 exempt. Also beside each code in the tabular there is a convention that looks like a circle with a backslash through it. This convention means that the code next to it is modifier 51 exempt. Code 45392 is the only code not listed in appendix E and that does not have this convention beside it.

28.   A - Category III codes are located between the Category II codes and Appendix A in the back of the CPT manual. Category III coding guidelines state that these codes are to be used before assigning an unlisted procedure code from category I codes.

29.   D - Medicare parts A is hospital insurance and helps cover inpatient care in hospitals, skilled nursing facility, hospice, and home health care. Medicare part B helps cover medically-necessary services like doctors' services, outpatient care, home health services, and other medical services. It also covers some preventive services.

30.   D - HIPAA has three rules; Privacy, Security, and Patient Safety. Standards for transmitting PHI are not regulated by HIPAA but the security of this information while it is being transmitted is. Once transmission rules are set HIPAA then set the standards on how this information should be protected.

31.   **D** - Following the hypertension table in the alphabetic index you would locate the term kidney. Beneath kidney are several stages of kidney disease available. Select the option describing stage I through stage IV, and this will provide you with code 403.00. In the tabular portion in the 5ᵗʰ digit box there is a notation stating to "Use additional code to identify the stage of chronic kidney disease (585.1–585.4, 585.9)".

32.   **D** - The correct open wound code is 881.10 because the wound has a foreign body. In the alphabetic index under the term "open, wound" there is a box that describe when to use the "complicated" option (this includes foreign bodies and infections). By selecting code 881.10 your choices are narrowed down to option B or D. Option B has an E code describing a fall resulting in striking a sharp object. This is incorrect because she struck the stove top (which was not sharp until it was broken by her fall). Option D's E code describes falling and striking an object and E920.8 describes being cut by broken glass.

33.   **B** - Burn codes always have no less than three codes: A burn code, a total body surface area code (948.XX), and an E code. You can have more than three codes but never less. Burn codes have the following rules (which can be found at the beginning of the ICD-9 book under general coding guidelines), always code one location to the highest degree (Ex. 1ˢᵗ and 2ⁿᵈ degree burns on the arm, only code 2ⁿᵈ degree). When sequencing burn codes always list the highest degree first (Ex. 1ˢᵗ degree burns to the face and 3ʳᵈ degree burns to the arm. List the arm burn first and then the face burn). Answer B is the answer because its codes describe the highest degree burn to each anatomical location, it sequences the burn codes in order of highest to lowest degree of burns, the 948 (TBSA code) has the correct calculation when using the rule of nine (4ᵗʰ digit burned to any degree; 9 x 5 = 45; fiver areas burned are head, arm1, arm2, leg1, leg 2; 5ᵗʰ digit describes only 3ʳᵈ degree burns which are head (9), leg1 (9), and leg2 (9). 9x3=27). The E code correctly describes the bonfire incident.

34.   D - Options B and C can be excluded because of code 650, which describes a normal delivery and not prolonged delivery. Option A and D only differ by one digit in the first code. Code 662.00 is incorrect because the 5th digit 0 is for "unspecified as to episode of care". 662.01 is correct because the 5th digit describes the patient having delivered. In option D the description of the second code, 659, is described as "elderly", and the tabular explains what "elderly" is considered. In this case the term "elderly" includes a pregnant woman who is 35 at the time of delivery. The 5th digit 5 accurately describes a woman's first pregnancy, as depicted in this question.

35.   A - Since both E codes, (E007.3 & E917.0), could apply to this situation it is difficult to narrow down the options by focusing on them. You can use the anatomical diagram in the CPT book if your book provides one, or you can use the common terminology provided in the question. The patient presents with pain in his distal middle finger. Look in the alphabetic index for the term fracture (the diagnosis), of the finger (the complaint of pain in the finger directs you here if you don't know what a "tuft" is). In the alphabetic indedx under "fracture, finger" you will be provided with a few options as well as a cross-reference (see also fracture, phalanx, hand). If you look up "fracture, phalanx, hand, distal" you will find code 816.02.

36.   B - Alcohol and drug *abuse* both are considered less severe than *dependence* since abuse can be stopped voluntarily and because abuse eventually escalates to dependence; Dependence is defined as "when one cannot voluntarily stop". The three-digit category 305 (in the tabular) also uses the description "nondependent abuse". Since the patient is stated as being dependent the 305 codes (like 305.71), would be incorrect. Since 305 codes are incorrect, option A and D can be ruled out. Also, since dependence encompasses abuse it is not necessary to code both the abuse and the dependence together, as it would be redundant; since option C codes both the alcohol dependence and the alcohol abuse (309.81 & 305.00), it is redundant and incorrect. Code just the dependence. Code 304 describes drug dependence. The 4th digit 4 describes the correct type of drug (amphetamine), and the 5th digit 1 accurately describes his use as "continuous". Code 304.71 (in option C), is incorrect because it describes an opioid instead of an amphetamine. Since the patient was not diagnosed with a general anxiety disorder code 300.02 would also be incorrect. Since the patient *is* experiencing anxiety as a symptom code 300.00 should be used. When the term "alcoholism" is looked up in the index you are led to code 303.9x in the tabular. The 5th digit 1 can be used here because his "long documented history" can be considered continuous use. Beneath the 303 category (in the tabular), there is also a notation that states to use additional codes to identify conditions, and lists "drug dependence 304.0 – 304.9, which should confirm your 304.41 code. Finally, code 309.81 accurately describes posttraumatic stress disorder (PTSD).

37.   C – Diabetic manifestations codes are all accompanied by a notation in the tabular that states to "use additional code to identify manifestation as", and then provides a list of codes to choose from. In our scenario the diabetic patient is experiencing an ophthalmic manifestation (AKA: manifestations of the eye), which is code 250.5 with a 5th digit. The 5th digit is located in a box above code 250.0 and beneath the three digit category 250. The 5th digit is used to distinguish the type of diabetes (type I or type II) and describes if it is controlled or uncontrolled. In our scenario the patient had type II diabetes (5th digits 0 and 2) and it is uncontrolled (5th digit 2). The full diabetes code should be 250.52, which limits your options to B & C. There is also a notation in the tabular beneath code 250.5x that states to "use *additional* code to identify manifestation as". Beneath this notation is a list of examples that can be used. These codes should be used following the 250.52, not before it. We know this because the notation states they are *"additional"* codes, as in a secondary. The list provided beneath code 250.5x includes "retinopathy 362.01 – 362.07", which is what the patient was diagnosed with. By flipping to this code range in the tabular and reading the description of each individual code we can determine that code 362.01 is the best option mainly due to the description beneath it, which includes "Diabetic Retinopathy NOS" (not otherwise specified). Directions beneath the four digit code 362.0x also states that these codes should be the *second* code in the sequence (code *first* 249.5x, 250.5x).

38.   A – This is true according the ICD-9-CM coding guidelines, (found in the beginning of the manual), under section I:B:7 which reads: Signs and symptoms that are associated routinely with a disease process should not be assigned as additional codes, unless otherwise instructed by the classification.

39.   **C** – The coding guidelines, (found at the beginning of the ICD–9–CM manual), specify the HIV coding rules in Section I; C; Chapter 1; A:1 and A:2:a–h. These guidelines state that V08 should be coded for asymptomatic HIV that has no documented symptoms, and may include the terms "HIV positive", "known HIV", and "HIV test positive". These are also extensive notations in the tabular portion beneath each of the HIV codes. Beneath code 042 is and excludes notation stating this code excludes asymptomatic HIV and to see code V08. Code 795.71 is used for unspecific pathology findings. The notation beneath this code states that "this code is **only** to be used when a test finding is reported as nonspecific. Asymptomatic findings are coded to V08....". The notation beneath code V08 verifies that this code should be used when no HIV infection symptoms or conditions are present. Code 079.53 has a notation beneath its three digit category (code 079) stating that codes starting with 079.XX are additional code meant to be used "in addition" to a primary code.

40.   **A** – The four digit category 692.7x indicates that codes starting with these four digits are cause by solar radiation (sunburn). Code 942.24 is a burn code caused by something other than the sun. Code 692.72 indicates a solar radiation burn causing an inflammation of the skin (dermatitis). In our scenario there is no documentation of inflammation though. Code 692.82 also describes dermatitis of the skin caused by radiation, but it is specific to rays other than solar (Ex. Tanning bed, ultraviolet rays). Code 692.76 accurately describes a second degree burn caused by the sun, without mention of inflammation (dermatitis).

HCPCS

41.　　C – Options A and D can be eliminated when comparing codes A6204 and A6252. Code A6204 states composite dressing is used and code A6204 states special absorptive sterile dressing is used (which is correct). When choosing between options B and C code A6219 meets the correct size requirements and also has an adhesive border.

42.　　D – Option A is a plaster cast so it is incorrect. Option B is for a pediatric cast and it states beneath the code that a pediatric cast is considered 0–10 years old, since the patient is 12 this code would be incorrect. Option C meets most of the description but it is for a splint and not a cast.

43.　　C – The correct answer is C for J9070. Neosar directs you to Cyclophosphamide 100 mg, which is a Chemotherapy drug used intravenously.
Answer A for J9011 is for Cytarabine 100 mg, which is not the correct medication.
Answer B for J7502 is for Cyclosporine oral medication, which is an immunosuppressive drug.
Answer D is J8999 and is a prescription oral chemotherapeutic drug and our patient is getting IV infusion.

44.　　B – The title for each code range is listed at the beginning of its code sets. Example: B codes start with code B4034 and right before this code is the B code set title "Enteral and Parenteral Therapy (B4000–B9999)". By turning to the first code in each code set listed you can locate the titles. Note that there is a difference between orthopedic foot ware and Diabetic footwear.

45.　　B – Code E1222 is the only option that states the leg rests are elevating (but not the detachable and swing away style). Although the other codes describe similar chairs we cannot code for something unless it is out right stated. Also, do not interpret that a "heavy duty wheelchair" or a "high strength wheelchair" is need because of the patient's size.

46.   C – The first thing to notice in this question is that no key components are provided. Because of that we can eliminate any code with the three key component requirements. Aside from the key components option A can also be eliminated because it is listed as a New Patient. This patient comes in weekly which means she is established. Option B requires key components that were not provided in this question so this can also be eliminated. Option D describes a code used for patient on blood thinners and is described in detail in the coding guidelines right above it. Code 99211 is listed under established patients and is one of the only codes in this section that a physician cannot use. This code is used for ancillary staff only (Ex. LPN, MA), which would apply in this circumstance since an LPN saw the patient. The description of this code also gives a hint, as it states this code is for visits that are "typically 5 minutes".

47.   D – Option A and and C are incorrect because the observation codes listed here (99218) are only for patients who are admitted and discharged on two different dates. Option B is incorrect because the description beneath this code states it, "requires these 3 key components: Comprehensive history, comprehensive exam, and moderate MDM". The physician performed only a detailed history and exam (not a comprehensive one). Although his MDM was of moderate complexity he did not provide the other two key components at the comprehensive level. Since the requirement of code 99235 is for al three key components to be met and only one was, option B is also incorrect. Option D is correct because codes 99234–99236 are used for patients who were admitted and discharge on the same day (see coding guidelines directly above code 99234). Code 99234 also requires that all 3 key components be met. In this scenario the first two key components (history and exam), met the requirement of being "detailed". The third key component (MDM) was also met *and exceeded*, since the physician went beyond straightforward/low complexity MDM and went to moderate MDM code 99234 can be used.

48.   D – If you were to compare the 99291 codes in A and C to the 99471 codes in B and D you would discover that the critical care code 99291, although good, is incorrect. The 99471 code is for initial critical

care for an inpatient pediatric (29 day old to 24 months). This code is more specific since the patient was admitted (inpatient) and is only 20 months old (pediatric). This then narrows down your options between B and D. B is incorrect because it includes a charge for the intubation, which according to the pediatric critical care coding guidelines, is a bundled service. The ICD-9 code 786.09 is also incorrect because it does not include the "acute" status. ICD-9 code 518.82 accurately describes "acute respiratory distress" and code 486 accurately describes pneumonia, unspecified.

49.   D - The physician performed three services: Stand by, resuscitation, and an E/M. By reading the descriptions of these codes and the guidelines provided for each code, you can determine which of them can or cannot be code in conjunction with one another. The coding guidelines for code 99360 state that the code "should not be used if the period of standby ends with the performance of a procedure". Initially you would think that this would then rule out the use of this code since Dr.Smith did end up rendering a procedure (resuscitation). However, there is a special notation in parentheses beneath code 99360 that states "99360 may be reported in addition to 99460, 99465 as appropriate". The next CPT code 99465 describes newborn resuscitation in the delivery room. This was the procedure that Dr.Smith provided, and is correct. The last code is 99460. This code describes the new born E/M that the physician provided. This code has no special notations or exclusions and is also correct. There is also a notation beneath code 99465 that states "99465 may be reported in conjunction with 99460". This means that all three codes can be used together.

50.   D - Comparing code 99387 to 99397: Both are for an annual wellness exam, and according to their descriptions, include age/gender appropriate history, exam, counseling (ex. smoking cessation), guidance, risk factors, etc. Code 99387 is for a new patient though and 99397 is for an established patient (both state the correct age). Since Mr. Johnson is stated as being an established patient, options A and B can be eliminated because of code 99387 (new patient). For options C and D you will then compare codes 99205 and 99215. Both of these codes describe an in-office E/M with a primary care physician. Code 99205 is for a new patient and also requires all three key components to be met. This code is incorrect because the patient is established (not new), and the MDM provided was only of moderate complexity (this code requires high

complexity MDM). Code 99215 is for an established patient though, and although the MDM for this codes states High and the physician only provided moderate, the codes description states that only 2 of the three key components need to be met. Since the Comprehensive history and exam were met, this code can still be assigned. This means option D, which includes both 99397 and 99215, is correct.

51.C – The answer to this question is found in the E/M coding guidelines under the 9th heading, labeled "Levels of E/M Service". These guidelines along with the guidelines found in this section under the heading "Time" (13th heading), explain that the 6 components 1) History 2) Exam 3) Medical Decision Making 4) Counseling 5) Coordination of Care 6) Nature of Presenting Problem or time (by itself), determines the level of an E/M service.

Anesthesia

52.   C - A 13-month-old child is over a year old so this rules out
options B. Option C is more specific than option A and meets our
description. Option D is incorrect because it does not describe a hernia
repair, but repair of the backside of the abdominal wall.

53.   A - The words *diagnostic* and *arthroscopic* are what leads you to
answer A. While answer B provides the correct anatomical description this
is also for an actual procedure (ex. Surgery), and not considered
exploratory for diagnostic purposes. Answer C describes an arthroscopic
procedure but it is also for a surgery (not diagnostic). Answer D
describes the actual procedure that the surgeon performed; however we
are only coding the anesthesia for the anesthesiologist in this question.

54.   C - The answer to this question is located in the Anesthesia coding
guidelines under the title "Time Reporting"

55.   B - The lining surrounding the heart is called the pericardium,
knowing this term helps to narrow down the options. Code 00560
accurately describes the surgery that was performed, however, this code
is meant to be used for patients over the age of 1, and does not include
the oxygenator pump. Code 00561, in answer B, states that this code is
for children under 1 year of age and includes an oxygenator pump. When
the age is specified in the code's description it is not necessary to add a
qualifying circumstance code (99100), re-stating the extreme age. Also
stated directly beneath code 00561, there is a notation stating "Do not
report 00561 in conjunction with 99100, 99116, and 99135". This
eliminates option D. Option C is incorrect because it does not describe
surgery on the pericardium, but on the great vessels of the heart instead.

56.   C - By recognizing the patient's age you can narrow down your
options to A or C (because of the qualifying circumstance code 99100
depicts extreme age, which is patients under the age of 1 and over the
age of 70). Qualifying circumstance codes can also be located in either
the Anesthesia coding guidelines and/or in the medicine chapter.
Knowing your medical terminology will also help you eliminate options
here. Option A describes a ten-*otomy*, the term "-otomy" means to cut
into, or to make an incision. Option B describes a teno-*desis*, the suffix –

esis means to remove fluid. In our question a repair was being done though. Code 01714 uses the term tenoplasty, and the suffix -plasty means to repair. Option C and D provide the same code, but D does not list the qualifying circumstance code 99100. Also the P modifier for *severe* asthma would be P3.

57.　　**B** - The answer to this question is found in the bottom half of paragraph two in the Anesthesia coding guidelines.

58.　　**A** - The qualifying circumstance codes (99140) is correct and narrows your choice down to options A or D. Both A and D have the same P modifier (P5), which is correct. Codes P5 and 99140 are correct because the patient is hemorrhaging and will bleed out and die without the operation; the surgery is also stated as "emergency". Option D describes an unspecified code but option A describes a tubal ligation, including laparoscopic procedures, which is what our scenario describes.

59.　　**D** - This question can be narrowed down by either the P modifier or by knowing some medical terminology. The P1 modifier describes an otherwise healthy individual and P2 describes an individual with a mild systemic disease (P modifiers are listed in Appendix A with all other modifiers). Since our patient was stated as "healthy" we can choose P1which will narrow down your options to A and D. Option A is close, but unspecified. Medical terminology reveals that option B describes an - *otoscopy,* which is the use of a scope in the ear. Option C describes biopsies of *intraoral* locations, and the term oral indicates the mouth. Answer D describes a biopsy (*-otomy)* of the eardrum (*tympanum).*

60.　　**D** - According to the Anesthesia coding guidelines under the heading "Time Reporting", anesthesia time begins when the anesthesiologist begins preparing the patient for the induction of anesthesia and ends when the anesthesiologist releases the patient from his care and is no longer in attendance. In our question this means the anesthesia time would be from 8:15am until 9:30am, which is 1hour and 15minutes.

61.　　**A** - When facing a longer more complex question like this one it is easier if you can eliminate some of your options. To eliminate two of your four options try to decide which P status modifier is correct (P2or P3) or compare codes 813.42 and 813.52, since each are appear twice in two different options. In this circumstance the P2 status modifier would be correct since both systemic diseases (diabetes and asthma) are well controlled and mild. The diagnosis code 813.42 is correct because the fracture is not stated as open (just the procedure is stated as open). When a fracture is not stated as open or closed it should be assumed as closed. By choosing both the P2 modifier and 813.42 diagnosis code, you can eliminate options B and D. When comparing option A and C look at the two anesthesia codes, 01830 and 01810. Code 01810 describes procedures for nerves, muscles, tendons, fascia, and the bursa, but not the bone. In this case code 01830 would be correct because it describes procedures performed on the distal radius bone (either open or with a scope). Additional ICD-9 codes 250.00 and 493.90 are also correct.

Integumentary

62.   B – According to the laceration coding guidelines (above code
12001, titled "Repair (closure)"), lacerations of the same depth and same
anatomical grouping should have their lengths added together and a
single code should be selected. Since the arm lacerations share the same
anatomical location (arm), and both are of the same depth (layered
lacerations), their length is added together (2.5 + 4 = 6.5 cm). Code
12032 is the correct code because it meets all three specifications: 1)
Length = 6.5cm 2) Depth = layered laceration 3) Anatomical Location =
the arm. The facial laceration would have a separate CPT code because it
has a different depth (simple laceration) as well as a different anatomical
location (face). Code 12013 is correct because it also meets all three
specifications: 1) Length = 3cm 2) Depth = Simple 3) Anatomical Location
= Face. According to the laceration repair guidelines "When more than
one classification of wound is repaired, list the more complicated as the
primary procedure and the less complicated as the secondary procedure,
using modifier 59." Option B correctly sequences the most complicated
code first (12032), followed by the least severe code (12013) with an
appended 59 modifier. ICD-9 codes 881.00, 880.00, and 873.42 also
correctly describe uncomplicated lacerations of the forearm, shoulder,
and face.

63.   C – The type of lesion divides the removal of lesions. Benign and
premalignant lesions have on set of removal codes and malignant lesion
removal has another set of codes. Each set of codes are also divided by
anatomical groupings, size, and the number of lesions being removed. In
this case the benign lesion of the scalp and premalignant lesion of the
neck will be coded with codes 17000-17250 and the malignant lesion of
the hand will be coded using codes 17260-17286. Sequencing our codes
from the most severe to the least severe, we will code our malignant
ablation first, followed by our pre-malignant, and finally our benign
ablation. Code 17273 is accurate because it is listed under the heading
"destruction, malignant lesions, any method". The anatomical grouping
starts at code 17270 (and includes the hand), and the specific code
17273 describes the size range 2.1cm – 3.0cm. Since our malignant
growth was 2.5cm, this code would be correct. The pre-malignant growth
and benign growth are both coded under the same heading, "destruction
benign or Premalignant Lesions" (code range 17000 – 17250). Code

17000 describes the removal of the *premalignant* lesion only, (it does not include benign lesions). There is no anatomical grouping here, just code s for the number of lesions being destroyed. Code 17003 is an add-on code that should only be used in conjunction with code 17000 (see notation beneath code 17003). This code should not be used with just another lesion destruction code (ex. 17273 & 17003). Code 17110 is used to describe the removal of the benign lesion of any location, up to 14.

64.   D - When faced with multiple codes that seem similar there are two ways to determine the correct code. Either choose the code that provides the most detail and remains accurate, or look up the terms in the alphabetic index. In this case looking up the terms "breast, cyst, puncture aspiration" in the index, will lead you to the code set 19000-19001. Code 19000 also provides the most detail because it has a specific anatomical location along with the correct description (a puncture aspiration).

65.   A - The easiest way to determine exactly what was done during this procedure is to look at the information at the very end of the operative note. Here we have the information that is most important to us: simple linear closure was performed; two stages (described as Mohs), were performed, and the number of sections in each stage are reported. According to the Mohs microsurgery guidelines, repairs are not bundled into the procedure and can be billed additionally. This means that the repair code 12002 (simple repair, 6.5cm, scalp), is correct and we can eliminate options C and D. Options A and B share three of the same codes, with one additional code in option A. So at this point the question is do you need code 17315 or not? Going through the Stages and sections: Stage I Section 1-5 is coded with 17311; Stage I Section 6 is coded with 17315; Stage II Section 1-5 (only 2 sections were performed in our scenario) is coded with; And code 12002 describes the simple, 3.5cm closure of the scalp.

66.   C - What the surgeon performed is a split-thickness graft. A split thickness graft uses the epidermis and a portion of the dermis from healthy tissue, removes it from its original location, but leaves a portion of it connected. The point of connection keeps the dermis and epidermis alive and is used as the pivot point for the graft. Option A describes something similar, but this is an adjacent tissue transfer (AKA: Flap Graft), which is usually thicker than a split-thickness graft, and which

usually involves transferring underlying tissues. . Option B describes an auto graft. An autograft can come from a donor site or from skin that is grown in a laboratory from the patient's own cells. This skin is then grafted to the defect. Option D describes a flap graft, which is deeper than just the dermis and can be rotated around a point, as opposed to just being flipped over.

67.   A - For this question you need to read each code's specific coding guidelines in order to determine which services are bundled. The 64400 code describes a digital block, however, this code would not be used because digital blocks are already built into the reimbursement for a laceration code and/or a subungual hematoma evacuation. This eliminates option B. Code 20103 states in the guidelines that this code is only used when a penetrating trauma has occurred, and this injury is not penetrating. In addition, this code describes *extensive* debridement, wound enlargement, major vessel ligation, etc. *Minor* debridement, ligation, and exploration are already bundled into a laceration repair code(see laceration coding guidelines), and since the question does not state that anything above routine (minor) work was done we cannot use code 20103.This eliminates options B, C and D. By default option A is the only choice left then. HCPCS modifiers F6 and F7 are correctly used to depict each individual finger. These modifiers can be found in Appendix A. Code 12042 accurately describes a layered finger laceration of 3 cm and code 11740 accurately describes a subungual hematoma evacuation.

68.   B - According to the lesion excision coding guidelines, (above code set 11400–11471), "Code selection is determined by measuring the greatest clinical diameter of the apparent lesion plus that margin required for complete excision (lesion diameter plus the most narrow margins required equals the excised diameter)".

69.   A - True. According to the laceration "Repair (closure)"coding guidelines (above code 12001), under the heading "Definitions, intermediate repair"...."Single–layer closure of heavily contaminated wounds that have required extensive cleaning or removal of particulate matter also constitutes intermediate repair".

70.   C - Knowing a little medical terminology will be how you determine this answer. The prefix *auto-* means "self", and an *autograft* is a graft

where the donor skin is from a different site on the recipients own body. The medical prefix *A* means "without" and the term *cell* refers to human body cells. The acellular graft uses both terms (a and cell) which would mean without cells, and an acellular graft is in fact without human cells because it is made of synthetic manmade materials. The medical prefix *allo* means "other". In the word allograft the prefix allo is referring to a graft from another human being. Finally, the prefix *xeno* means "foreign". In the case of a xenograft it is referring to the graft being from a foreign species (Ex. Pig).

71.   C - Code 97597 and 97602 are found in the medicine chapter and describe active open wound care (Ex. Decubitus ulcers). Beneath the Active Wound Care Management coding guidelines there is a notation that states, "For debridement of burn wounds, see 16020-16030). This eliminates options A and B. Code 16030 is used to describe the removal of dead tissue on second-degree (partial thickness) burns. Not only is the degree of burn different, but in our scenario there was no mention of tissue removal, only cleansing and incisions. This eliminates option D. Code 16035 describes an Escharotomy (note the suffix *-otomy* means to "cut into"). An Escharotomy is a procedure performed on healing *third* degree burns. Incisions are made into the thick dead tissue to keep underlying nerves and vessels from being injured or constricted. Code 16036 is an add on code which is used in conjunction with code 16035. This add on code should be used for each additional incision. So code 16035 describes the first incision and code 16036 x2 describes the second and third incision.

Musculoskeletal

72. **D** - Option A describes an open procedure instead of an arthroscopic one, so this option can be eliminated. Option B is arthroscopic, but the procedure is described for the hip instead of the knee, it is also used to describe a transplant (instead of a repair), so this too is incorrect. The difference between C and D is the word "and" vs "or". In our question the patient had both the medial *and* lateral meniscus repaired, so code 29883 would be correct.

73. **B** - Open fractures do not always utilize "open fracture treatment" codes. In the ICD-9 an open fracture means that the skin has been broken. In the CPT book "open" and "closed" are term used to refer to the type of treatment. If the patient is taken to the operating room and an incision is made in order to visualize the fracture, this would be considered "open" treatment. If the physician manipulates the fracture without creating an opening it is considered "closed treatment". In this scenario the patient has an open fracture but "closed fracture treatment" is utilized. Codes 25574 describe an "open treatment" and so options A and C are incorrect. Option B and D both have the same CPT codes, but different modifiers. Any procedure with a 90 global period can be broken down into three portions: Pre-operative assessment and/or decision for surgery; Surgical (the actual procedure); Post-operative follow-up care. In this scenario the fracture care has a 90 global period and can be broken down into these three portions. The E/M service is considered the pre-operative evaluation *and* the decision for surgery since the patient has to give consent to proceed, because of this the E/M should have the 57 modifier appended. The 57 modifier describes "decision for surgery" (see appendix A). The 25 modifier is also appended to the E/M because of the additional procedure (12031, laceration repair). The fracture care is considered the "surgical" portion of the package and so modifier 54 is appended to the fracture care code. Modifier 54 is used to describe "Surgical care only" (see appendix A). The HCPCS modifier RT is used to describe which arm was receiving care. (See appendix A for RT modifier's full description).

74. **D** - Knowing medical terminology will help you choose the answer for this question. Specific medical suffixes usually fall under a specific heading, such as: the suffix *-otomy* which means to "cut into", is usually

under the heading "incisions". The suffix *-ectomy* which means "to remove", is usually found under the "excision" heading. The suffixes *-plasty* and *-pexy* mean to repair, and so terms with these suffixes usually fall under the heading "repair", such as Scapulo*pexy*. If you don't know medical terminology you can also try looking up the term scapulopexy in the index, which will lead you to code 23400. Code 23400 is under the heading "Repair, Revision, and/or Reconstruction".

75.   B - The procedure being performed in this question is a trigger point injection. Codes 64400 and 64520 are used to describe nerve blocks. These are injections involving the nervous system, instead of injecting muscles, as was done in our scenario. This eliminates options A and C. Codes 20552 and 20553 both describe trigger point injections and both codes include multiple injections. Code 20552 describes 1 or more injections into 1 - 2 muscles, and code 20553 describes 1 or more injections into 3 or more muscles. Since only one muscle was being injected multiple times, code 20552 is correct.

76.   A - Per. Paul Cadorette and the American Medical Association article titled "Coding Guidance for Anterior Cervical Arthrodesis", "When a spinal fusion (arthrodesis) is performed, the first thing a coder needs to recognize is the approach or technique that was utilized. With an anterior (front of the body) approach to a cervical fusion the incision will be made in the patient's neck, so the key terms to look for are platysma, esophagus, carotid and sternocleidomastoid. These structures will be divided and/or protected during dissection down to the vertebral body. After dissection, the procedure can proceed in one of three ways:
   a. When the interspace is prepared (minimal discectomy, perforation of endplates) then 22554 would be reported.
   b. When a discectomy is performed to decompress the spinal cord and/or nerve root(s) report 22554 for the arthrodesis along with 63075 for the discectomy procedure.
   c. When a partial corpectomy (vertebral body resection) is performed at C5 and C6 report CPT code 22554 for the arthrodesis with 63081 and 63082. Two codes are reported because the corpectomy procedure is performed on two vertebral segments (C5 and C6). *CPT codes 63081-63091 include a discectomy above and/or below the vertebral segment*, so code 63075 (discectomy) would not be reported if performed at the C5-C6 interspace.

Once the decompression procedure has been completed, a PEEK cage can be placed within the interspace or a structural bone graft can be fashioned to fit the vertebral defect created by the previous corpectomy. Insertion of the PEEK cage would be reported with a biomechanical device code 22851. This code is only reported one time per level even if two cages are placed at C5-C6. When a structural bone graft is used, determine whether it is an allograft (20931) or an autograft (20938). The bone graft codes are only reported one time per procedure and not once for each level. Finally, the physician will place an anterior plate with screws (22845) across the C5-C6 interspace to stabilize the area of fusion".

Some guidance on coding such procedures can also be located in the Spine (vertebral column) coding guidelines (above code 22010).

77.   B - In this scenario each answer has the identical codes, only with different modifiers. Modifiers can be referenced quickly on the CPT book's front cover, and can be found with a full description and guidelines in Appendix A. Guidance for this question really comes from looking at the guidelines above the two codes that were provided. According to osteotomy guidelines (above code 22206) when two surgeons work together as primary surgeons performing distinct parts of an anterior spine osteotomy each surgeon should report their distinct operative work by appending modifier 62 to the procedure code.

78.   D - "Fracture care", as described by code 25600, includes pain management, fracture reduction (if necessary), and initial stabilization. Since the patient came into the physician's office with a cast already in place we can deduct that the patient already received initial fracture care. Coding 25600 would be inappropriate then, because the patient was already charged for fracture care once. The physician performed only a cast application, as described by code 29075. Option C is also incorrect. Although the physician did remove the prior cast, it was never specified to be a *full arm* cast. I was most likely a short arm cast, but you cannot draw assumptions when coding.

79.   D - According to arthroscopy coding guidelines (found above code 29800), surgical arthroscopies include diagnostic arthroscopies,(they are bundled), this means a diagnostic arthroscopy cannot be billed in conjunction with a surgical one. If a diagnostic arthroscopy turns into a surgical procedure, the surgeon can only bill for the surgical portion. This would then eliminate code 29805, which appears on both options A and

B. Code 29819 has the correct description for the removal of a foreign body, in the shoulder, by arthroscopy. Modifier 78 would not be appended because the patient is past his 90 day global period, and there is no mention that this is the same surgeon who performed the initial surgery.

80.   **B** – Most CPT books (like the one published by the AMA and required by the AAPC for the CPC Exam), have diagrams with detailed descriptions accompanying these codes. If your CPT book has their diagrams, reading the detailed captions will direct you to the correct code selection. In this scenario the diagram provided for code 28290 describes the correct "medial eminence of the metatarsal bone" being removed, but since there is no mention of the Kirschner wire used to stabilize the joint, this code is incorrect. The diagram for code 28294 describes a bunionectomy but describes a tendon transplant being an integral component of this procedure, and this was not performed in our question. The diagram for code 28298 describes the removal of the "medial eminence" and the Kirschner wire stabilization, but also includes the *additional* removal of several bone wedges from the base of the phalanx. Our scenario describes the surgeon cutting into the foot, moving tendons and other structures out of the way, removing the medial eminence, stabilizing the joint with Kirschner wire, and closing the patient up. This is procedure is best described by code 28292, and is accurately depicted in the accompanying diagram.

Respiratory, Cardiovascular, Hemic and Lymphatic, Mediastinum, and Diaphragm

81.   **B** – For this question we will look at the operative note first and explain what is being done, then we will look at each answer and dissect the codes. The operative note describes two coronary artery bypass grafts, one graft is a vein and the other is an artery. The second paragraph describe how the patient was opened up, the dissection performed to reach the heart, and the harvesting of a mammary artery that will be grafted to the heart. The third paragraph describes the harvesting of a femoral popliteal vein that will be used for a graft on the heart. The fourth paragraph describes sewing the artery and vein to the existing heart vessels prior to cutting the damaged portion out. The fifth paragraph describes the patient being placed on a machine that will

breathe and beat their heart for them (cardiopulmonary bypass). Once this is done the surgeon cuts out the damaged heart vessels and the ends of the new vessels are sewn to the exposed ends (anastomosis) of the remaining heart vessels.

A chest tube is also place for fluid drainage during recovery. Paragraph six then describes the patient being closed up and sent to recovery. In our scenario the opening and closure of the patient are part of the main procedure and should not be reported separately. Anastomosis is part of vessel grafting and is also bundled into the main procedure code. Cardiopulmonary bypass is considered an integral part of open heart surgery and should not be coded separately either. Placement of a chest tube is only billed when it is not part of a larger procedure. Since a larger procedure was performed (CABG) the chest tube will not be coded here. Vessel harvesting may or may not be coded in addition to the primary codes depending in the type of vessel being harvested and the primary procedure's coding guidelines.

Option A: Code 35600 correctly describes the harvesting of an upper extremity artery that will be used as a graft for the heart, however, in our scenario the mammary artery was harvested and according to the CABG coding guidelines (above codes 33510, 33517, and 33533) the procurement of any artery (except one from the arm) is already included in the graft codes and should not be reported separately. This means that code 35600 cannot be used here. Code 35572 describes the harvesting of a femoralpopliteal vein. The same CABG coding guidelines also tell us that a harvested vein is included in the grafting codes and should not be coded separately unless it is a femoralpopliteal vein. Since the vein that was harvested was a femoralpopliteal vein we are directed to use the additional code 35572. Code 33533 is also the correct code and accurately describes a single *artery* bypass done on a heart vessel (in this case the artery is the mammary and the heart vessel is the descending aorta). Code 33517 is correct because it describes a single *vein* being grafted when an artery is also being grafted during the same operation. Code 32551 correctly describes the placement of the chest tube, however, the code should not be use because the placement of a chest tube is bundled into (or included in) a CABG. This is why there is a notation beneath code 32551 that says: "separate procedure". Code 36825 describes a procedure that joins two vessels (that are not on the heart) by a method *other than* anastomosis. This was not performed in our scenario and should not be coded. Code 33926 describes cardiopulmonary bypass being used during the repair of an artery that links the lungs and heart (pulmonary artery); (see code 33925 for the common descriptor), this was not performed here and should not be coded.

Option B: Code 33533 is correct for a single artery graft to the heart. Code 33517 is an add-on code for 33533 and accurately describes a single vein graft to a heart vessel when an artery graft is also performed. According to the CABG coding guidelines code 35572 should be used for femoralpopliteal vein harvesting. The procurement of the mammary artery, anastomosis, cardiopulmonary bypass and chest tube placement are all bundled with the CABG codes and should not be coded separately.

Option C: Code 33510 describes a vein being grafted to a heart vessel when *only* veins are being used. Since an artery and a vein were both grafted we would use code 33517 instead. Codes 33533 and 35572 were already established as correct (see description under option A rational). Code 32551 (chest tube) is included in the CABG grafting procedures and should not be coded separately. Code 36821 describes anastomosis performed on vessels outside the heart for dialysis purposes, which was not performed here and should not be coded.

Option D: Code 33510 is the only incorrect code for this option. Code 33510 describes a vein being grafted to a heart vessel when *only* veins are being used. Since an artery and a vein were both grafted we would use code 33517 in addition to the artery code 33533 instead of code 33510.

82.   D – Option A and C share the same description and provide different age brackets and options B and D share the same description and provide different age brackets. Option A and C are both for kids five years and under. Since our patient is 50 we can eliminate options A and C. The difference between the remaining options B and D is the description "tunneled" catheter verses a "non-tunneled" catheter. A tunneled catheter is one that enters the body, tunnels under the skin, and exits the body in a different place. A non-tunneled catheter is one that enters the body and resides in the point of entry. Our scenario describes the catheter entering and residing in/near the point of entry (subclavian). Most CPT books (like the AMA's professional edition)

provide diagrams of these procedures above or below the corresponding codes and include a short description of the process. The diagram for code 36556 specifically states "the catheter tip must reside in the subclavian, innominate, or other iliac veins..."

83.   A - The *right* lung has *three* lobes so when *two* lobes are removed it is called a *bi*-lobectomy and when the whole lung is removed it is called a total pneumonectomy. The *left* lung only has *two* lobes (so the heart has room to expand). When one lobe of the left lung is removed it is called a lobectomy and when two lobes are removed it is called a total pneumonectomy (because the whole lung is being removed). Because our question describes the left lung, code 32482 is incorrect. Code 32482 describes a bi-lobectomy, but in the case of the left lung, that would be the entire lung (total pneumonectomy). A pleaurectomy is the removal if the pleura, not the lung or its lobes (32310). In our scenario a total pneumonectomy was performed, and it was in an open fashion (not laparoscopically– 32663).

84.   A - In our scenario the surgeon took a biopsy of tissue from the mediastinal space using a scope. Noting that a scope was used we can eliminate options C and D because these are codes describing open procedures. The difference between option A and B is the approach used. A thoracoscopy of the mediastinal space (32606) approaches through the chest wall and then manipulate the scope from the thorax into the mediastinal space. Mediastinoscopies (39400) approach by making an incision under the sternal notch at the base of the throat and enter directly into the mediastinum.

85.   C - Reading the notations below several of these codes is how you will choose the best option here. Code 31237 states beside it "separate procedure", which means if it was performed at the same time as another procedure then it cannot be coded and is bundled into the primary procedure. This means option A and B can be eliminated because this code is listed. In addition, option B can also be eliminated because code 31201 describes an open ethmoidectomy and in our scenario it was performed endoscopically. In option C and D code 31255 is correct and accurately describes an anterior and posterior removal of the ethmoid sinuses. Code 31295 (in option D), was also performed and correctly coded, however, beneath the code there is a notation that it should not

be used in conjunction with code 31267 (which is one of the correct codes in the answer too). Code 31267 describes the nasal polyp removal, and since we know that it cannot be used in conjunction with code 31295, option C is correct. Option C can also be deduced by reading the multiple notations beneath code 31256. The third notation states "for anterior and posterior ethmoidectomy (APE), and frontal sinus exploration, with or without polyp(s) removal, use 31255 and 31276".

86.   D - In this question the surgeon placed a permanent dual chamber pace maker. Code 33240 in option A describes a cardioverter-defibrillator instead of a pacemaker, this rules out option A. Option B has the correct code 33208 to describe the pacemaker placement with leads in both the atrial and ventricular chambers. Codes 33225 and 33202 are incorrect though, because according to the pacemaker coding guidelines (found above code33202) *and* the notations below code 33208, transvenous placement of electrodes is included in code 33208. Codes 33225 and 33202 should only be used when additional electrodes are placed. Code 33213 in option C describes only the battery portion of the unit being placed. The notation below this codes states that if electrodes are coded to use 33202 or 33203 (not code 33217). Option D accurately describes the placement of both the pacemaker generator and the two transvenous electrodes.

87.   B - According to the endoscopy coding guidelines (found above code 31231), "A surgical sinus endoscopy includes a sinusotomy (when appropriate) and diagnostic endoscopy.

88.   C - Code 36217 in options A and B describes the selective catheter placement to the third order, but in the wrong vascular family (36217 is for thoracic or brachiocephalic). The correct family is the "lower extremity" (where the femoral artery is located). This eliminates options A and B. Code 36245 includes the common descriptor belonging to code 36247, and includes the correct "lower extremity" vascular family. Options C and D provide the correct catherization code but provide different ultrasound codes. Code 37250 is used to describe the actual procedure, while code 75945 is used to describe the supervision of the procedure and the interpretation of the ultrasound report/images. Since we are billing for the actual service that was rendered, code 37250 is correct.

89.   A – The "indirect" view refers to looking at the larynx in an indirect fashion, such as a reflection. A "direct" view refers to looking directly at the larynx.

90.   D – Code 38308 describes surgery done on a lymphatic channel instead of a lymph node, so this code is incorrect. What the surgeon performed was a biopsy of a lymphnode in the armpit (axillia). Code 38500 describes a biopsy, but is for a superficial one. The procedure describes dissection through the fascia (this covers the muscle), and the full excision of the entire lymphnode (which was then sent to pathology). Code 38510 has the correct common descriptor, which begins at code 38500 and reads "Biopsy or excision of lymphnode(s);". The unique descriptor of this code describes the location being on the neck instead of the axillia though, so this code is also incorrect. Code 38525 accurately describes the biopsy/excision of the deep axillary nodes.

Digestive

91.   D – The term esophagogastroduodenoscopy (abbreviated EGD) describes the viewing of the esophagus (esophago), the stomach (gastro), and the duodenum (duodeno), with a camera/scope (oscopy). Option A describes an esophagoscopy, which is a scope performed with a biopsy, but does not move farther than the esophagus. Option B describes an examination of the upper GI, but does not describe the tissue sampling. Option C correctly describes an EDG, but a tissue sample is not the same as obtaining cells through brushing or washing, since the physician actually took a sample, this code is also incorrect. Option D, code 43239, uses the same common descriptor in code 43235, but the unique descriptor (beside code 43239) correctly describes the tissue biopsy. There may also be a diagram of code 43235 which describes a scope going through the esophagus, stomach, and to the duodenum. This diagram may also help narrow down the options to C and D.

92.   C – By reading the Endoscopy coding guidelines (above ode 45300) and the Colonoscopy "coding tip"(above code 45355) we can learn that a sigmoidoscopy is an endoscopy that advances to the descending colon but no further, and a colonoscopy is an endoscopy that advances past the splenic flexure , into the cecum, and may go as far as the terminal ileum. The physician had planned to advance into the cecum, which means he was going to perform a colonoscopy. He chose not to perform the entire colonoscopy though, due to unforeseen circumstances (fecal impaction). According to "coding tip" coding guidelines (above code 45355 in the AMA Professional Edition), we should still code for the colonoscopy and then add modifier 53 to indicate that the entire procedure was not completed. This means that code 45378 with a 53 modifier is correct.

93.   A – The operative note describes the open repair of a unilateral inguinal hernia with mesh placement (Marlex patch). Code 49505 accurately describes the repair of a unilateral inguinal hernia (open) and includes the mesh placement (see hernia coding guidelines above code 49491 which state in the fourth paragraph "With the exception of the incisional hernia repairs (49560–49566) the use of mesh or other prostheses is not separately reported"). Beneath code 49507 there is a notation stating that if a simple orchiectomy (removal of a testicle) is also performed during the hernia repair, that codes 49505 and/or 49507

should be used in conjunction with code 54520. In our scenario an orchiectomy was *not* performed though, so using codes 49505 or 49507 with code 54520 would be incorrect. This eliminates options B and D. Code 49568 describes the use of mesh during the repair of an incisional or venteral hernia only (our hernia was inguinal), and beneath this code is a list of the CPT codes it *should* be used in conjunction with. Code 49505 is *not* included in that list. Also, remember the hernia coding guidelines (above code 49491) states that "with the exception of the incisional hernia repairs (codes 49560–49566) the use of mesh or other prostheses in not separately reported".

94.   A - This information can be found above code 40800 under the heading "Vestibule of Mouth". If looking up the term "vestibule" in the index you are told to see "mouth, vestibule of". Looking up this term should lead you near code 40800, where you will find the description of a vestibule (above the code).

95.   A - The digestive system is made up of two portions: the alimentary canal, and the accessory organs. The alimentary canal starts at the mouth and ends at the anus. The alimentary canal is also what food passes through during the digestive process. Parts of the alimentary canal include the mouth, esophagus, stomach, and intestines. Accessory organs are organs that aid in digestion but do not come in direct contact with the food. Accessory organs include the gallbladder, liver, and pancreas. This information is not listed in the CPT book. Since the AAPC allows notations to be made in your books, it is a good idea to make a notation regarding this beside your digestive system diagram (prior to code 40490 and following code 39599).

96.   C - Codes 42826, 42831, and 42836 are all used to describe when *either* a tonsillectomy *or* an adenoidectomy are performed. When the two are performed together code 42821 would be reported. This is because items such as anesthesia, opening the patient up, and closing the patient may be bundled with the surgery code. Since the surgeon would only need to make one incision and close the patient up only once, even when removing two organs, the removal of both are bundle under the same code. Choosing both a tonsillectomy code (42826) and an adenoidectomy code (42831 or 42836) the surgeon would be reimbursed twice for services he only performed once (ex. Incision, dissection, closure).This

then eliminates options A and B. Code 42821 also does not need modifier 50 appended because the code is used for a total tonsillectomy and total adenoidectomy, not a unilateral one. Had this been a unilateral procedure it would either state it in the description or there would be a notation below the code regarding the use of modifier 50. ICD-9-CM code 463 correctly describes acute tonsillitis, which is an inflammation and not the same thing as an abscess, which is described by code 475. Code 474.0 is incorrect because it has a 5th digit available which was not used. Coding guidelines state that if a 5th digit is available it must always be used, thus code 474.0 is incorrect, but code 474.0*2 is* correct.

97.   A – The operative note describes an endoscopic percutaneous gastrostomy tube placement. Code 43246 describes this correctly (see code 43235 for the common descriptor). Modifier 62 is needed because Dr. Smith only performed the tube placement. If he were to charge code 43246 with no modifier he would be reimbursed for the EDG as well. Since Dr. Brown performed the EDG potion of this code he would also charge code 43246-62. This way each physician is reimbursed half. Code 49440 describes a non-endoscopic gastostomy tube placement. Code 43752 is also a non-endoscopic procedure. Code 43653 is a laparoscopic procedure, which means they created a small incision through which the camera entered the body; instead of an endoscopic procedure, which enters the body through an existing opening (ex. mouth).

98.   C – Code 43756 is not used for evacuation of stomach contents, but for things like bile studies. The duodenum is also where the stomach and small intestine connect, which was not mentioned in our scenario. Code 43752 describes the placement of a permanent tube that is meant not for evacuation, but for introducing nutrients or medication into the body. Code 43753 is the correct code. Gastric intubation is the introduction of a tube into the stomach and aspiration is synonymous with evacuation. Some CPT books (like the AMA's professional edition) have an added diagram of this code and a detailed description that includes key terms like: "large-bore gastric lavage tube" and "evacuation of stomach contents". It also includes examples of why this code would be used, including poisonings. Option D describes a gastric intubation as well (which was performed here), but this code it is only performed for diagnostic purposes, not to correct an already known problem (which would be therapeutic).

99.   **B** - Endoscopies (not laparoscopies) performed in the digestive chapter run between codes: 43200-43273; 44360-44397; 45300-45392; 46600-46615; and 47550-47556. There is a convention to the right of these codes that looks like a target, and they are there to indicate that moderate sedation is already included in that particular CPT code, and therefore cannot be coded separately. The definition to this convention can be located in the front of the CPT book (Introduction, page xii in the AMA's Professional Edition), or at the bottom of each page in the CPT book. While the majority of the codes have this convention beside them there are some that do not, for example, codes: 45300; 45330; 45331; 46600-46615; 47550-47556. All codes that include moderate sedation are also listed in the back of the CPT book in Appendix G. By referencing Appendix G, you will also see that codes 45300; 45330; 45331; 46600-46615; and 47550-47556 are not listed as including moderate sedation.

100.   **A** - According to the Bariatric surgery coding guidelines (above code 43770), a lap band adjustment consists of changing the restrictive band's diameter by injecting or aspirating fluid through a subcutaneous port. Because this description is beneath the laparoscopic heading the procedure code for this should also be under the laparoscopic heading. Option B (43886) is an open procedure which would require sedation and an incision. The code's description also describes a revision to the actual port, not the lap band. Option C (43842) is also an open procedure which would require the patient to be in an operating room. This code describes the *placement* of a restrictive device, not the *revision* of one that is already in place. Option D (43848) is also an open procedure code and describes the revision of the restrictive *procedure,* and not the revision of a restrictive *device.* Code 43771 in option A correctly describes a laparoscopic procedure (through an existing port) for the revision of an already placed restrictive device.

Urinary, Male Genital, and Female Genital Systems, and Maternity Care and Delivery

101. **D** - This question describes a patient with renal calculi (kidney stone) and the procedure that breaks the stone into smaller pieces, which is called lithotripsy. The term "lith" means stone and the term "trip" means to break. Code 50590 describes the use of the lithotripsy wave machine (C-Arm image intensifier) to send shock waves from the outside of the body in (extracorpeal). This code may also have a diagram describing lithotripsy in more detail. Radiology codes, such as 74425 and 76770 were not utilized here. Code 50081 describes a percutaneous procedure that enters the kidney from the outside (likely using a needle), and then retrieves the stone, without destroying it. Codes 50060 & 50130 both describe open procedures. The suffix -otomy means to cut into. The terms nephrolithotomy and pyelolithotomy both mean to cut into the kidney (nephro and pyelo both mean kidney) and remove a stone (lith). Since neither an open procedure nor incisions were made in our scenario, these codes are also incorrect.

102. **B** - Code 57155 describes the placement of small radioactive elements, which are left in the patient for the course of treatment prescribed and then later removed. Code 57156 describes the insertion of a vaginal radiation afterloading apparatus for clinical brachytherapy. This code should be used for the placement of vaginal cylinder rods, or similar afterloading devices. This procedure is also typically performed in a post-hysterectomy patient. An "afterloading apparatus" is described as a technique where the radioactivity is loaded after proper placement of the apparatus has been confirmed. The rods (or afterloading device) should have an access port on the outside of the body which can then be hooked up to an external machine which can deliver either high dose or low dose rate brachytherapy. Although the patient recently had a hysterectomy it does not state exactly how long ago or by whom, and since we cannot assume anything modifier 58 is not applied.

103. **D** - Our scenario in this question is describing a vasectomy. Option A describes the "ligation" of the vas deferens, which is one form of a vasectomy that ties off, or strangulates, the vas deferens in order to block the exit of semen. This procedure does not require any dissection or removal of the tube though, as is described in our scenario. Option B and C are used to describe a vasectomy reversal. As the two suffixes

imply;   -ostomy means to create a permanent opening (as in opening a ligated vas deferns) and   -orraphy means to repair. Depending on the version of the CPT book you own, you may be able to locate common terms like these in the front of the manual (ex. AMA professional edition on page xiv). Code 55250 in option D accurately describes the performance of a vasectomy, unilateral or bilateral.

104.   B – Option A is a laparoscopic procedure and in our scenario an open procedure was performed. Option C describes a total nephrectomy (removal of the whole kidney) along with the removal of part of the uterus and a rib resection (which is a removal of a portion or all of the rib). In our scenario only a portion of the kidney was removed, and there is no mention of the uterus or ribs being removed (only dissected through). Code 50290 in option D describes the removal of a perinephric cyst, which is an accumulation of fluid in a cyst like mass between the kidney and surrounding capsule. There is no mention of a perinephric cyst in our scenario, so this is also incorrect. In our scenario a portion of the kidney (which contained the tumor), was removed in an open fashion. The term nephro– means kidney and the suffix -ectomy means to remove. This is accurately described by code 50240, Nephrectomy, partial. Commone prefixes, Root Words, and Suffixes may be located in the beginning of your CPT book.

105.   B – For twin gestation, report the deliveries separately with no modifier on the first and modifier 51 on the second. If all maternity care was provided, report the global obstetric (OB) service for the first infant (that is the antepartum/postpartum care), and report the appropriate delivery–only code for the second infant using modifier 51. This means that code 59618, which describes a cesarean delivery, after a previous cesarean delivery, and a vaginal birth attempt (according to the coding guidelines above code 59610), and includes the antepartum and postpartum care would be correct for the first infant. Code 59620-51 would be correct for the second infant born since antepartum and postpartum care was not provided twice (just once to one patient). Modifier 51 indicates multiple procedures are being billed and this is not the primary procedure. Modifier 22 on the single code 59618 would not be correct because a single procedure requiring more work was not performed, what was performed was two individual procedures requiring the standard amount of. Code 669.71 is correct Code V27.2 is correct

and states that this code is meant for use in the maternal record and not the infants. Code V91.01. Code 651.01 accurately describes the patient as having twin gestations and delivering during this encounter, this code also includes a notation indicating that a code from range V91.00 – V91.99 is needed. In this scenario code V91.01 is the correct choice. Code 644.21 accurately describes the patient as having premature labor (prior to 37 completed weeks of gestation) and delivering during this encounter. Code 669.71 accurately describes the complication of vaginal labor resulting in a cesarean delivery. Three digit category V27 indicates these codes are to be used as a result of delivery in the maternal health record. Code V27.2 accurately describes two babies born alive. Code V31.1 would be incorrect because this code is meant for the infant's health care chart, not the maternal record.

106.　　A – According to the maternity care and delivery guidelines (prior to code 59000), in the middle of the fourth paragraph, " When reporting delivery only services (59409, 59514, 59612, and 59620), report inpatient post delivery management and discharge services using Evaluation and Management service codes.

107.　　C – PSA is an antigen tested in males to detect prostate cancer. Any reading over 10 is considered high. In this scenario the patient is having a prostate biopsy performed to determine is he has prostate cancer or benign prostate hypertrophy. Option A describes a needle or catheter being place by the transperineal approach, for the purpose of entering small radioactive elements into the body to kill cancerous cells. Option B also describes a transperineal approach with the use of a needle for a prostate biopsy, however, it also describes a sterotactic template guided saturation sampling. A saturation biopsy is an alternative technique utilized by urologists to detect cancer in high risk patients by taking multiple samples (usually 30 or more). This code also includes the imaging guidance so a 70000 code (like 76942) should not be coded in addition to it. Code 55705 in option D is used to describe a biopsy taken by an open procedure. This would include an incision and repair. Code 55700 accurately describes a prostate biopsy, by needle or punch, by any approach (including retroperineal). Notations beneath this code also direct you to code 76942 for ultrasonic guidance if performed.

108. A – A hydrocele is a pathological fluid filled sack within the scrotum. This question describes a bilateral hydrocelectomy of the tunic vaginalis. What makes this question more difficult is that medicinally a hydrocelectomy and a hydrocele repair are sometimes used synonymously. Code 54861in option B describes a procedure removing both of the Epididymis tubes and has no mention of a hydrocele, so this easily rules out option B. Code 55000-50 in option C describes a procedure performed on both tunic vaginalis, but it is a puncture aspiration (a hole punched with a needle to drain the fluid), so this can be ruled out as well since our physician performed an incision and dissection. Code 55060 in option D and code 55041 in option A comes down to the type of procedure and its details. Code 55060 is a "bottle type procedure, also known as "Andrews Procedure". This procedure requires a 2-3cm incision in the hydrocele sack near the superior portion (or top) and requires tacking the cut edges around the cord structures, leaving the everted sac open. Also, when choosing between these two codes note the heading each one is under. Code 55041 is under the "Excision" heading and code 55060 is under the "Repair" heading. In a hydrocele excision (code 55041) the majority of the sac is removed. In a hydrocele repair (code 55060) the sac is cut open and the edges are tacked back. The procedure is also stated as being a "hydrocelectomy" and the suffix -ectomy means to remove (similar to the excision).

109. B – Code 51797 should not be used without its primary code. Beneath code 51797 it states that this code should be used in addition to either code 51728 or 51729. Since options A and C utilized code 51797 without its primary code these two options are incorrect. Code 51729 utilizes the common descriptor next to code 51726 but also include its own unique descriptor "with voiding pressure studies", making its full description "Complex cystometrogram (ie. Calibrated electronic equipment); with voiding pressure studies". Code 51797 is an add-on code describing the "intra-abdominal" portion and notes that it should be used in addition to code 51729. This would make the codes in options B and C both correct. According to the Urodynamics coding guidelines (above code 51725), if the physician did not provide the equipment and is simply operating it and interpreting the report then modifier 26 should be added to these codes. Since they physician in our scenario is utilizing hospital equipment and not his own adding modifier 26 would be correct.

110. **C** – Code 58976 describes the transfer of an already *fertilized* egg within the fallopian tube, in our scenario the eggs are *unfertilized* though, and they are being harvested from the ovarian follicles (not transferred). Code 58672 is a laparoscopic procedure (instead of a percutaneous one), and describe the *repair* of a fimbio. Code 58970 correctly describes the harvesting of the unfertilized eggs from the ovarian follicle with the use of an ultrasonic guided needle. Beneath this code there is a notation stating code 76948 is to be used for radiological supervision and interpretation. Code 58940 is used to describe the removal of one or both ovaries.

Endocrine, Nervous, Ocular, and Auditory Systems

111. **B** -The only way to find the answer for this question is to use the anatomical diagrams in the auditory chapter. There are two diagrams in the auditory chapter that have pictures of the ossicles. One diagram depicts a tympanoplasy (codes 69635 - 69646), and the other diagram depicts a tympanostomy (codes 69433–69436). Although the ossicles are not labeled individually, they are labeled "auditory ossicles". Using the picture of the three ossicles you can then look at a second diagram of the ear, located in the auditory coding guidelines (prior to code69000). The same picture of the three ossicles is shown, but this time they are labeled individually as the Incus, Malleus, and Stapes. Writing the terms hammer, anvil, and stirrup beneath these three diagram may be useful when taking the CPC Exam, (this is an AAPC approved notation; These diagrams are in the AMA's Professional CPT Edition, 2012).

112. **C** – Code 62160 in options A and D describe the use of a neuroendoscope, which was not mentioned in our scenario, so these options are in correct. Options B and C are very similar, but code 61210 describes a *burr* hole and code 61107 describes a *twist drill* hole. The difference is that a burr hole is created with an electronic drill and a special bit, and the twist drill is a manually operated hand tool that is twisted to make a hole. Code 61107 also describes a puncture method (performed with a needle) instead of an incision made with a scalpel.

113. **A** - Code 63040 is for a laminectomy (–ectomy meaning removal, of the lamina) and a partial facetectomy (–ectomy meaning removal, of the facet), with nerve decompression, and with *or* without removal of herniated a disc. Choosing option A as your answer would be done by focusing on key phrases in this question, such as: "the ligamentum flavum, *lamina*, and fragments of a ruptured C3–C4 intervertebral disc were all *removed*" and "the surgeon *removed* a portion of the *facet*", and "to *relieve the compressed nerve*". Code 63075 in option B describes an *anterior approach* (approaching from the front of the body), since our scenario describes a *posterior* approach (approching from the back of the body), we know this code is incorrect. In addition, this code also describes the removal of a herniated disc, which would require the sternocleoidmastoid muscle and carotid artery being retracted, the removal of the disc, and a T shaped graft from the ilium. These things

were not described in our scenario though. Code 63081 describes a vertebral corpectomy, which is the removal (-ectomy) of the vertebral corpus. A corpectomy would require the surgeon would incise the dura and locate denated ligaments and section them. Closure could or could not include a graft. Code 63170 in option D describes a laminectomy (removal of the lamina) with a myelotomy (myle meaning muscle and -otomy meaning to cut into). This procedure includes the laminectomy describes in our scenario, but in addition the surgeon incises the dura and the outer white matter of the spinal cord, which was not performed.

114.   C - A keratoplasty means to repair the cornea (kerato means cornea and -plasty means repair). A keratoplasty of the anterior lamellar is a surgical procedure that removes the corneal stroma down the descemet's membrane. This is a partial thickness graft that preserves the two inner most layers of the cornea. Keratomileusis (kerato meaning cornea and mieusis meaning to carve or shape), is a type of lasik eye surgery. Here the ophthalmologist creates a flap of corneal tissue, then uses a laser to remold the original cornea, and then the cornea flap is replaced. Keratophakia (kerato meaning cornea and phakia meaning lens), is the procedure described in our scenario (which uses a donor lens). Keratoprosthesis (kerato meaning cornea and prosthesis meaning an artificial substitute) is the replacement of the cornea with an artificial one that is bio-engineered.

115.   C - The endocrine system codes start with code 6000 and end with code 60699. The first heading in the endocrine chapter is "thyroid gland". Following the codes through the chapter you come to code 60500 and the next (and final) heading (directly above this code), which reads "Parathyroid, Thymus, Adrenal Glands, Pancreas, and Carotid Body". The only organ not listed in the endocrine chapter is the Lymph nodes, which are part of the hemic-lymphatic system located at the end of the 30000 codes.

116.   C - The coding guidelines above code 69990 (operating microscope) state that it should not be coded in addition to multiple codes. Among the codes listed is code range 65091 - 68850. Since both code 67107 and 67101 are within that code range the operating microscope should not be coded with them. This eliminates options B and D. Code 67101 and code 67107 differ little, but code 67107 does include

the terms "sclera buckling" and "with or without implant". The band placed around the eye causes sclera buckeling and in scenario there was not an implant. This code is also further explained in some CPT books that contain diagrams.

117.   C - The neurosurgeon performed a crainiotomy (he cut into the skull; Craini means head and -otomy means to cut into), and drained an *intracerebellar* hematoma (which is a collection of blood). Code 61154 describes the burr hole accurately, but no craniotomy, it also describes the evacuation of the hematoma correctly, but it is missing the location (intracerebellum). This means you can eliminate options A and D. Code 61315 correctly describes the scenario, "Craniectomy *or crainiotomy* for *evacuation of hematoma*, infratentorial; *intracerebellar*. Although the neurosurgeon did create a burr hole during the procedure, notations beneath code 61253 state that "if burr holes or trephine are followed by a crainiotomy at the same operative session, use 61304-61321; do not use 61250 or 61253".

118.   D - The main difference in these codes are the specific nerve being decompressed. Code 64702 is the description of a nerve decompression for a finger or toe. Code 64704 is also a nerve decompression, but for a hand or foot. Code 64719 is the code used for a nerve decompression of the ulnar nerve of the wrist. Code 64721, which is described in our scenario, is the nerve decompression of the *median nerve*, also known as carpal tunnel surgery.

119.   B - The procedure performed is a repair to a fistula in the *round* window. Code 69666 and code 69667 both accurately describes this procedure, but code 69666 is performed on the *oval* window and code 69667 is performed on the *round* window. Options A and C can be ruled out, because they describe they utilize the oval window code instead of the round window code. There are no notations beneath code 69667 excluding modifier 50, and coding guidelines state that if a procedure is not stated it as a bilateral operation (or is not specified in the guidelines), then it is assumed to be uni-lateral. Since code 69667 is not noted as being bilateral we must assume it is unilateral. Since the surgeon performed this procedure on both ears modifier 50 would be correct. Code 69990 has a list of CPT codes it cannot be coded in conjunction with (see Operating Microscope Coding Guidelines above code 69990),

however, code 69667 is not one of them, therefore, coding 69990 in addition to code 69667 is correct.

120.   B – Code 60512 is an add-on code and beneath it is a list of codes it *can* be "added onto". This list includes code 60260 (option A), code 60240 which is a total thyroidectomy (Option C), and code 60500 (Option C). Add-on codes are always added onto a primary procedure code and are never to be used as a primary code or as a single code (see General Coding Guidelines, Add-on Codes, pg. xi, AMA Professional Edition 2012).

Radiology

121. **C** - The full CPT code has both components, technical and professional, and if the physician did not perform both components he cannot be reimbursed for them both. The TC modifier is used to depict the technical component, which is what the radiologist often utilizes. Modifier 26 is the professional component, which is what the physician should append to his CPT code. Modifier 52 is used when a physician must terminate a procedure or attempts an entire procedure but has unsuccessful results. A full description of modifiers 26 and 52 can be found in appendix A. Modifier TC in a HCPCS modifier and should be referenced in the HCPCS book.

122. **A** - According to the chart provided above code 74176, the guidelines above that, and the notation beneath code 74178, code 74178 is a standalone code. Guidelines state "do not report more than one CT of the abdomen or CT of the pelvis for any single session". Using the chart the last box across the top should be selected (in bold) "74170 CT of the Abdomen without contrast followed by with contrast (abbreviated WO//W Contrast)", and the top box on the side should be selected, "72192, CT of the Pelvis without contrast (abbreviated WO Contrast)". Following both selections to the point where they meet you end up in the last box in the first (non-bold) column, which contains code "74178". Notations beneath this codes state, "Do not report 74176 – 74178 in conjunction with 72192 – 72194, 7415 – 74170".

123. **C** - The radiologist took 3 views of the patient's *facial bones*. The Water's view (oblique anterior-posterior), anterior-posterior view, and lateral view. Code 70100 is a view of the mandible only, which is located in the jaw. Code 70120 describes 3 views of the mastoid, which is located near the ear and attached to the temporal bone. Code 70150 accurately describes three views taken of unspecified facial bones. Code 70250 describes skull bones, and not facial bones, being viewed.

124. **A** - The "Aorta and Arteries" coding guidelines (above code 75600) state that a diagnostic angiography may be reported with an interventional procedure when performed together under specific circumstances. One such circumstance is when a prior report is recorded in the medical record but states there is inadequate visualization of the anatomy. These guidelines also state modifier 59 would need to be appended to the diagnostic radiological supervision and interpretation. To find this information you would use the alphabetic index and look up the term "angiography". The index would direct you to "see aortography". Looking up the term "Aorta, aortography" would lead you to code 75600, and the guidelines above it.

125.B – For the bone biopsy, code 20225 accurately describes a percutaneous, deep bone, biopsy. Code 20245 describes the same thing; only open instead of percutaneous (requiring an incision instead of a needle). Code 38221 is a biopsy of the bone marrow (not the actual bone). Beneath code 20225 the notations state to use either code 77002, 77012, or 77021 for radiological supervision and interpretation. Code 77012 accurately depicts the CAT scan (computed tomography). Code 76998 describes the use of an ultrasound instead of a CAT scan, and code 73700 is used when a *diagnostic* CAT scan is being taken, not a procedural one.

126.C – High dose radiation (HDR) brachytherapy (AKA: internal radiation) is a type of radiation that uses high doses of radioactive sources, places them remotely, usually for short periods of time, and then removes them. The unit that holds the radioactive sources is called an afterloader and they are delivered to the tumor through channels (usually a catheter). HDR brachytherapy is different from intracavitary brachytherapy, which places lower dosed radioactive sources for longer periods of time. Codes for intracavitary brachytherapy are not determined by the number of channels used, but the number of radioactive sources delivered (see coding guidelines above code 77750). Interstitial radiation is similar to intracavitary radiation except that instead of placing the radioactive elements in a body cavity they are placed within body tissue. Code 77762 (A) describes intracavitary radiation and code 77777 (D) describes interstitial radiation. Code 77790 (B) is used when charging for the handling of the radioactive elements and equipment *before and after* the procedure. Code 77786 (C), accurately describes the procedure of high dose radiation using a remote afterloading device with 2–12 channels (3 were used in our scenario).

127. A – There is little difference between codes 78451 and 78453. Code 78451 is done by SPECT and includes attenuation correction and code 78453 is a planar type image. In our scenario code 78451 is correct. This rules out options B and D. According to the Radiology Cardiovascular System coding guidelines, (above code 78414), when a myocardial perfusion study using codes 78451–78454 or 78472–78492 is performed in conjunction with a stress test, then the stress test should be coded in addition to the study using codes 93015 - 93018. In our scenario code 93016 is correct because the physician did not provide the interpretation and report (the cardiologist did).

128.C – The fluid at the back of the fetuses' neck is also known as the nuchal fold or the nuchal translucency. When this is too thick it is an indication the fetus may have down syndrome. Option A describes an ultrasound for both the fetuses and the mother. In our scenario only the fetuses are being evaluated though, so this eliminates option A. Option B also includes a maternal evaluation, so this too is incorrect. Option C correctly describes the first trimester, fetus evaluation only, is specific to the nuchal translucency, and includes a transabdominal approach. Add-on code 76814 is also correct when reporting multiple gestations, (per. notations beneath code 76814, it should be used in conjunction with code 76813 when reporting multiple gestations). Option D describes a *re*-evaluation to confirm a prior finding. In our scenario there is no mention of a prior screening.

129.A – Code 3598 accurately describes the injection of a contrast material (radiopaque iodine) into a central venous access device (Hickman's catheter). This cods also includes the fluoroscopic imaging and report. According to the notations beneath code 36598 you are not to code 76000 in conjunction with it, so option C is incorrect. These notations also state that if you are looking to code "complete diagnostic studies, see 75820, 75825, 75827", it does not say you *must* use them in addition to this code though. When reading the Radiology "Vein and Lymphatic" coding guidelines (above code 75801), it states that if a "Diagnostic venography is performed at the same time as an interventional procedure it is NOT separately reportable if it is specifically included in the interventional code descriptor". Also, in our scenario there is not clear indication that a full vein study was done, only a CVAD check. Since code 36598 includes the fluoroscopic imaging and report there is nothing else to report.

130. A – The radiology coding guidelines (prior to code 70010), in the last paragraph, states that a signed written report is an integral part of the radiologic service or interpretation.

Pathology and Laboratory

131.C – When coding a panel every test in that panel must be performed or that panel cannot be coded. Every code listed in our scenario is listed beneath code 80053 except the TSH (which is coded using code 84443). Code 80053 also has an additional test for Albumin listed. Since an Albumin level was not ordered we cannot use code 80053, even with a 52 modifier. This eliminates option A. Option B lists *total* calcium levels being ordered instead of *ionized* calcium levels, so this is incorrect. Option C is correct because every test listed beneath code 80047 was ordered. In addition to 80047, the lab tests not listed are accurately coded individually. Option D seems like a good option because it does accurately capture each test listed in our scenario, however, code 80047 captures a larger number of tests while still being correct and utilizes fewer codes overall which makes this the better option. When give the option between choosing a panel or listing each test individually, you should select the panel.

132.A – Only a gross examination was performed here. There is no mention of a microscopic examination, so even though an ovary is not specifically listed beneath code 88300, it is the only code that does not include the microscopic examination.

133.B – Appendix "A" has a full description of each modifier and how it should or should not be used. Modifier 99 should be used when a single CPT code has two or more modifiers appended to it. Modifier 99 could be used in place of the multiple modifiers and the specific modifiers could then be listed elsewhere on a claim form. Modifier 76 is meant to be used on a service and/or procedure code, not laboratory codes. The use of modifier 76 eliminates option A. Modifier 91 is meant to be used on laboratory codes, and is used to when a test is purposely ran more than once on the same day. Modifier 91 should only be appended to the second test and beyond though, and not to the first test performed (like in option C). Option B is correct because it lists each test once without a modifier and then the second and third time each of those tests were ran modifier 91 was appended, indicating that it was actually performed multiple times in one day. If option D was billed, the insurance company would pay each test only once and then deny the second and third time the test was run as a "duplicate charge", this is because the 91 modifier was not appended to indicate they were not duplicates.

134. **B** - Code 81005 is used for an analysis of the urine for things like protein, glucose, and bacteria. This is often performed by way of a dip stick and may be accompanied by a microscopic examination. This is not what is described in our scenario, and eliminates options A and D. Code 81025 accurately describes a urine test that provides a positive or negative result, in this case, pregnancy. Code 84702 and 84703 are both used when testing for the growth hormone hCG. Code 84703 is a qualitative test and tests if hCG is present or not. Code 84702 is a quantitative test, usually run to confirm a pregnancy, and provides a specific level of the hormone, such as 12500 mIU/ml.

135. **D** - The first drug test done on the random urine sample is done for all four drugs and is considered a qualitative test (only giving a negative or positive result). Code 80100 is incorrect because it involves the use of mobile and non-mobile phases, which were not mentioned in our scenario. Code 80101 is a simple immunoassay type test which is used for single drug class, but can be used multiple times to indicate several drug classes. This is not the correct code though, as our scenario specifically states a multiplexed drug screening kit was used. Beneath code 8010 there is a notation that states, "for qualitative analysis by multiplexed screening kit for multiple drugs or drug classes, use 80104". In our scenario four different drug classes are being tested for, using a multiplexed screening kit. A multiplexed screening kit can test for multiple drug classes at once, so the use of this code for multiple drugs being screened for is correct. Code 80104 could be used multiple times if multiple "kits" were being used. Modifier 91 (if it were correct), would be applied to the second, third, and fourth test to avoid a "duplicate" denial from the insurance company. According to appendix "A", modifier 91 may be used when a laboratory test is repeated on the same day to obtain multiple test results. The two drugs that had a positive result were then tested in a *quantitative fashion.* Although code 80102 is usually used to confirm an initial drug test, it is used to confirm the presence of the drug in a more sensitive fashion and may give the specific drug (ex. If a barbiturate test is positive code 80102 may confirm the test was ran correctly, had the correct retention time, and that the barbiturate was specific to Amytal). In our scenario this is not the type of secondary test that was run though. A quantitative test, such as codes 82205 and

83925, is used to determine the specific *level* of the drug being tested. Codes 82205 and 83925 can also be located by using the chart (located right before the Pathology and Laboratory coding guidelines). Using the chart's farthest column labeled "quantitative" and locating the specific drug in the left hand column, the two meet in the appropriate boxes containing these codes.

136.C - CBC stands for complete blood count. Codes for a CBC are 85025 and 85027. These codes can be located by looking up "CBC" in the index and following the cross -reference. The codes descriptions in the tabular index explain that a CBC includes Hgb (hemoglobin), Hct (hematocrit), RBC (red blood cell count), WBC (white blood cell count), and platelet count. Not included in a CBC is hCG (human chorionic gonadotropin), which is a human growth hormone that is elevated in pregnancy and often tested for to confirm the stage of pregnancy.

137.B - Code 89255 is used to describe a fertilized egg being prepared for implantation into a woman's uterus. Code 89258 is the code used when taking an embryo and preserving it by freezing, (the medical prefix cryo- means cold). This is what the technician did in our scenario. Code 89268 describes the egg (oocyte) being fertilized with the sperm to form a zygote. And code 89342 is a code that is used when an embryo is already frozen and is simply being stored.

138.D - A glucose tolerance test (GTT) requires the patient to have a blood draw prior to the glucose, they then receive glucose in some form, and then have their blood drawn at intervals to determine how their body metabolizes the glucose. Code 82951 is the correct code for this test and includes the pre-glucose blood draw, the glucose dose, and the three blood draws following the ingestion. Code 82946 is also a tolerance test, but it is for glucagon and not glucose. Code 82950 is a glucose test that is very similar to the GTT, but does not require a blood draw prior to the glucose and is usually only checked once, 2 hours after the glucose dose is received. According to appendix "A" modifier 91 should not be used when a test is re-run due to a testing problem. Because the laboratory caused the issue the patient's insurance should not be charged for two tests.

139.C– Code 80047 (in options B and D) has both carbon dioxide and sodium, but it contains *ionized* calcium not *total* calcium. This eliminates options B and D. Option A has the individual codes for carbon dioxide, total calcium, and sodium, but lists no panel codes. By default option C would be correct. Each code listed beside option C (80048, 80053, and 80069) are panel codes and each one has all three of the elements listed (carbon dioxide, total calcium, and sodium).

140.A – This is true in many tests (not just hCH). Generally a qualitative test is a simple test that usually produces a positive or negative result. A quantitative test is usually a more sensitive method for testing or confirming a substance and will provide results such as specific level of the substance being tested for.

Medicine

141.B – The diagnosis coding should include code 873.41 for the simple laceration of the cheek, code 880.09 for multiple lacerations of the upper arm, and code V01.5 for the exposure to rabies. According to the laceration coding guidelines (above code 12001), any laceration located in the same anatomical grouping that requires the same depth of repair may have their lengths added together for a single code selection. This means that the two lacerations on the arm (same anatomical location) which had the same type of repair (both were layered repairs) can have their lengths added together (1cm + 4cm = 5cm) and a single code can be selected (code 12032). The single laceration on the face was a simple repair which is found in the code range 12001 – 12021. The correct anatomical grouping that includes the face are codes 12011 – 12018, and the single code for our length is code 12013 (2.6cm – 5.0cm). Because this is a secondary procedure we append modifier 51. Next we focus on the rabies injection. Choosing the correct code here will depend on the coding guidelines and on the difference between an immune globulin *immunization* and a toxoid *vaccination*. An immune globulin is a substance that is administered in order to *prevent* an illness and provides passive immunization. Passive immunization protects the body for a small period of time by introducing antibodies into the blood stream that were donated by another human's plasma. A toxoid vaccination is the introduction of a dead virus into the blood stream. This introduction stimulates the immune system to produce its own antibodies and provide long term protection. In our scenario a toxoid *vaccination* was administered. Code 96372 in option A is a code that is used for a SQ or IM injections, but is specific to therapeutic (curative), prophylactic (preventative), or diagnostic injections only. The notation beneath this code specifies that for vaccines/toxoids see codes 96365, 96366, 90471, or 90472. Of these four codes listed two are for IV infusions (96365 and 96366), and are incorrect. The coding guidelines for remaining codes (90471 and 90472), are titled "immunization administration for vaccines and toxoids", and are located above code 90460. According to these coding guidelines (second paragraph) codes 90471 (option C) and code 90472 are only for individuals over the age of 18 (our patient is 5). These guidelines also direct you to use 90460 and 90461. The description of code 90460 is accurate to our patient's age, includes the physician's counseling of the parents, and describes the vaccination toxoid administration. The first sentence of these guidelines (still above code 90460) also informs you to use a code from the 90476 - 90749 range in addition to code 90460. The additional code to describe the substance being injected is not code 90375 (options A and D), because an *immune globulin* was not administered, a *toxoid* was. Code 90675 is within the specified code range of 90476 - 90749 and describes an IM rabies vaccination. According to the Vaccine/Toxoid coding guidelines (above code 90476), in the third paragraph, you are told that this code (90675) is only for the substance, that the administration code should come from code range 90460 - 90474 (in our case code 90460), and that modifier 51 should NOT be appended to the substance code.

142.A - The physician did not perform the actual EKG but ordered another individual to run it, so the physician cannot charge code 93000, which includes reimbursement for performing the test. In this scenario code 93010 would accurately describe the report and interpretation. This eliminates options B and D. Normal saline (NS) was also infused for 1 hour and 45 minutes. According to the hydration coding guidelines (above code 96360), normal saline is included in the 96360 and 96361 codes and can be charged by a physician who is supervising, but not actually performing, the hydration. Code 96360 may only be reported once for the initial hour and each increment of time beyond that must utilize the add-on code 96361. Although the 96361 code description says it is for each additional hour, a notation beneath the code states that code 96361 may be used for time increments of 30 minutes or greater if the total infusion time is at least 1 hour and 30 minutes (or longer).

143.D - Reading the "End-Stage Renal Disease Services" coding guidelines (above code 90951) is the key to selecting this code. According to these guidelines code 90960 is used when providing these services in an outpatient setting (like a physician's office), not for home dialysis. This eliminates option A. Code 90966 is for home dialysis and correctly describes our patient's age bracket (20 and older), however, according to the coding guidelines these codes cannot be used for patients receiving services for less than a full month (30 days). This eliminates option B. Code 90970 is the correct code, but per. the description of this code, and per. the coding guidelines, this code should be reported for each day of service outside any inpatient setting. This eliminates option C and makes option D correct. The physician performed dialysis on the 15th - 18th (4 days), and then resumed dialysis on the 25th - 31st (7 days). For the month the physician should charge 11 days.

144.**D** - There are a lot of coding guidelines (2 ½ pages) that belong to codes 93279 - 93299. These guidelines give specific directives about when these code can and cannot be used, what other codes they can and cannot be used in conjunction with, time specifications, and device descriptions. In our scenario the patient has an implantable cardioverter-defibrillator (ICD) that has implantable cardiovascular monitoring (ICM) functionalities. According to the ICM coding guidelines "when ICM functionality is included in an ICD device the ICM data and the ICD data are distinct and so the monitoring process is considered distinct (coded separately). The coding for the ICD (defibrillator) includes 90 days of remote analysis for a dual lead device and one face-to-face encounter for programming purposes. Code 93295 is used once every 90 days for reporting remote analysis of a dual lead defibrillator, and code 93283 is used to describe the in person encounter for programming and adjustments made to the dual lead defibrillator. Codes for the ICM include 90 days of remote analysis. Code 93297 is used to describe remote analysis of an ICM and is reported once for every 30 days. The correct use of this code would then be 93297 x3 (30 x 3 = 90days). Although the physician also provided an in person encounter for the ICM, according to the second paragraph of the coding guidelines, "A physician may NOT report an in-person and remote interrogation device evaluation when they are performed during the same period". These guidelines go on to say that when both remote and in-person services are rendered in the same time period to only bill the remote services. In addition, there are also notations beneath codes 93297 and 93290 that state they should not be coded in conjunction with one another.

145.**B** - According to the ophthalmology coding guidelines a comprehensive ophthalmological service includes history, general medical observation, external examinations (lids, sclera, conjunctiva, etc.) and ophthalmoscopic examinations (slit lamp/Goldman 3-mirror lens), gross visual fields, and basic sensorimotor examinations (vertical prism bars, function of ocular motor system, etc.). It also often includes cycloplegia (drug used for dilation of pupils), and tonometry (measures intraocular pressure; "17 mm on each eye"). It always includes diagnostic and treatment plans (dx: cataracts and macular degeneration; tx: continued vitamins and surgery) as well. In addition to this description the coding guidelines also specify that "itemization of services, such as slit lamp examinations, keratometry, routine ophthalmoscopy, retinoscopy, tonometry, and motor evaluation is not applicable". This means that since our scenario meets all the requirements to code an established, comprehensive, ophthalmological service, that we cannot use additional codes (such as 92060 or 92081), as they are already bundled into our service code (92014).

146.A - The rules regarding "separate procedures" and the 59 modifier can be located under the third title in the medicine coding guidelines, titled "Separate Procedure". These rules apply to all CPT codes, (not just those in the medicine chapter), and the stipulations are repeated in several other coding guidelines as well.

147.B - The simplest way to code this would be to code for one day and then just multiple that for the number of visits in the month. When coding for a single day you would use code 99601 as the initial peritoneal infusion code and code 99602 for the additional hour. These codes would be used on all three days the nurse visits and code 99509 would be added on once each week for the additional services performed on Fridays. Code 90966 would not be correct because this code is only for physician use (not nurses). Code 99512 is also incorrect because this code is for hemodialysis and not peritoneal dialysis. Beneath this code there is even a notation stating that if coding for home infusion of peritoneal dialysis to use codes 99601 and 99602. The number of Mondays, Wednesdays, and Fridays in the month add up to 13. It would be incorrect to code one initial infusion code (99601) and the rest of the visits as code (99602 x25), because code 99601 states that it should be used "per visit". This means that code 99601 should be used for each individual date of service with the add-on code 99602 for each date of service. (99601 x13 and 99602 x13). In a month there were also 4 Fridays and so code 99509 would be coded as 99509 x4.

148.D -Code 93923 includes what is described in our scenario, but also has additional studies as well (ex. 3 levels instead of 2 levels of plethymograohy volume were taken, 3 or more oxygen tension measurements are taken instead of 2. Etc.) This eliminates options A and B. Code 93922 accurately describes what is performed in our scenario. Requirements for using this code are also given in the coding guidelines (above code 93880), under the heading "Noninvasive Vascular Diagnostic Studies", in the 5th paragraph titled, "Limited studies for lower extremity". These guidelines stipulations include items stated in our questions, such as " ABI's (ankle/brachial indices) being taken at the posterior (back) and anterior (front) lower aspects of the tibial and tibial/dorsalis pedis arteries; Plethymography levels; Oxygen tension reading, etc. The notation beneath code 93922 also states that if a single extremity, (instead of both), are being studied to append modifier 52 to the procedure code.

149.B – Code 91010 is a manometric study, but it is of the esophagus (throat) and/or where the stomach and esophagus meet (gastroesophageal junction; gastro meaning stomach and esophageal meaning the esophagus). Code 91020, (Gastric motility), is also a manometric study, and accurately describes our scenario. The term "gastric" (or gastro), means the stomach and the word "motility" is a biological term referring to the ability to move. In this case it is referring to the ability of food to move through the stomach. Code 91022 is similar to code 91020, except the anatomical location is different – it is studying the duodenum. The duodenum is the first portion of the small intestine, and code 91022 is the study of movement through this. Code 0242T is a category III code located between category II codes and Appendix A in the back of the CPT book. Code 0242T is also similar to a motility study but this particular code utilizes a wireless capsule and studies not only the stomach but also the small and large intestines through the colon.

150.B – To the left of each code are listed any coding conventions. Conventions each have their own meaning, which can be found with a short description at the bottom of each page or in their full description at the front of the CPT book. The coding convention that looks like a lightning bolt means "FDA approval pending". Codes 90664, 90666, and 90667 each have this convention listed beside them. Code 90665, which is located out of numerical sequence and can be found beneath code 90668, does not have this coding convention listed beside it.

34504940R10084

Made in the USA
Lexington, KY
08 August 2014